No-Choice Theory

No-Choice Theory

—ɷ—

A SIMPLIFIED SCIENTIFIC
ANALYSIS OF THE ISSUES OF
FREE WILL AND DETERMINISM

Ahmad Safavy, PhD

Copyright © 2017 Ahmad Safavy, PhD
All rights reserved.
Printed in the United States of America.

No part of this book may be used, copied, or reproduced in any way whatsoever without written permission from the Author. Exceptions are brief excerpts and quotations used in critical comments and articles.

Where required, references to credits for figures are noted in the relevant figure legends and cited in the related *NOTES* section.

First published in 2017
ISBN: 1543207065
ISBN 13: 9781543207064
Library of Congress Control Number: 2017902715
CreateSpace Independent Publishing Platform
North Charleston, South Carolina

To

Princess Soody

and

Dr. Davood Safavy, MD

"Everything in the Universe is within you. Ask all from yourself"

Rumi (Persian mystic philosopher and poet, 1207-1273)

Acknowledgements

THE SUPPORT AND ENCOURAGEMENTS OF my family, Kamellia, Shirin, and Seena, have been the "determining factor" in my achievements. I thank them as I am driven because of them, always.

I would like to gratefully acknowledge the important contributions from all those who have enlightened me with their advice, guidance, and suggestions, through the many years of my search for what I have now found.

Valuable discussions with Professor Ryoichi Kawai on quantum mechanical issues are also acknowledged.

Table of Contents

Preface · xiii
Introduction · xvii

Chapter 1   *Occam's Razor* · 1
Chapter 2   *The Mother of All Beginnings* · · · · · · · · · · · · · 3
Chapter 3   *The Building Blocks of our Tangible World* · · · · · · · 15
Chapter 4   *Chemical Bonds and Molecules* · · · · · · · · · · · · · 39
Chapter 5   *Higher-Order Structures and Molecular Shapes* · · · · · · 55
Chapter 6   *Peripheral Factors in the Formation of Molecules* · · · · · · 64
Chapter 7   *The Feat* · 75
Chapter 8   *Structure-Function Relationships* · · · · · · · · · · · · 99
Chapter 9   *Genes, Brains, and Behavior* · · · · · · · · · · · · · · 107
Chapter 10 *Are We All Set?* · · · · · · · · · · · · · · · · · · · 123
Chapter 11 *Don't Blame the Weatherman: It's a Chaos Out There!* · · · 136
Chapter 12 *A Strange Science* · · · · · · · · · · · · · · · · · · 145
Chapter 13 *The Synthesis* · 167
Chapter 14 *Translation* · 199

Name Index · 209
Subject Index · 211

Preface

THE FIRST POINT I SHOULD want to mention here is that this book may have the title and appearance of a natural science book, and as such, may seem somewhat daunting to those who either are not much fond of physical sciences, or have never had a chance to take a science course, or both. Well, it should not. It has been written in a way that, if read with the intention of understanding it, it should need no science background. In fact, it may give the non-scientist reader a chance to learn a little bit of some useful science that may come handy sometime. All the science topics covered here have been described in lay language. So, if you are interested in the main subjects of the book, that are Determinism and whether or not we have Freewill, just relax and read on. Rest assured that by the time you finished the book, every piece will have fallen into its own place and you will have understood it as good as someone with a science background.

The book attempts to prove that our Universe works though a deterministic and a cause-and-effect driving mechanism. To arrive at this conclusion, it has adopted a step-by-step approach to utilize the available scientific knowledge. The start of the journey is with the currently accepted theory for the birth of our Universe, the Big Bang theory. Taken as a beginning for everything, the book looks at the stages of the world's development following the Big Bang, and shows along the way that an interconnected cause-and-effect phenomenon, and therefore, a deterministic nature of the world, may be the actual working mechanism. Based on this hypothesis, the book then guides you through the remaining chapters to arrive at its final conclusion on the ancient but ever-curious issue of human Freewill.

It is absolutely important to keep in mind, however, that the material presented in this book is just a touch on the surface of Determinism and Freewill, which is intended to present you with yet another way of analyzing and thinking about these issues. For instance, if a deterministic relationship between the genome, the brain structure, the environment, and the very occurrence of a certain Event is being discussed, it could go only so far as to stimulate your thoughts and imagination for drawing a logic-based judgement of your own. It would then be up to you to decide whether or not they could make any sense, and thus, the book's message could be used for the adoption of a new way of looking at the World. There is absolutely no way for anyone to present you with a clear-cut and actual picture of the "genes-brains-environment" interaction that brings about that particular Event. The real mechanisms of this and other processes that turn the wheels of this Universe are way too complicated to be wholly illustrated in a book or in a picture, or demonstrated as a model in a laboratory experiment. All we could do, rather, is to extrapolate from evidence and try to dissect the issue using our power of thinking and imagination, as well as our scientific knowledge, however limited it might be. And the hope should be that "extrapolation from evidence" may be able to compensate for that limitation.

With all due respect to both genders, and to those who have rightfully chosen to switch, I have only used the old-fashioned version of the third-person personal, possessive, and prepositional pronouns, *"he"*, *"his"*, and *"him"*, respectively, in this book and in those cases where no definite subject is intended. This was for ease of typing only (as I am not a speedy keyboard puncher) and also the fact that following the *Old English* style would be usually easier and more "automatic" for most of us. Bottom line: Strictly no ignorance or disrespect is intended.

Throughout the text, lifetimes of people are given as two parenthesized numbers (birth year-death year) and only at the first mention of each name. For people who are still with us, naturally only the birth years are shown. Time periods older than around 2000 years are followed by the letters "BCE" for "Before Current Era".

In some instances, for the non-human subject names, and when emphasis on the significance of the reference is to be reflected, the first letters of the names are capitalized (for example Universe and Nature). For "Life" as an independent and absolute entity, again the first letter is capitalized. For "life", when meant that of plants' and animals', I have used the term "biological life". The reason is that I do believe in the *universality* of Life and the principle that nothing is dead, and on the contrary, everything is very much alive. That is, of course, a separate subject and I just suffice to say only so much in here to help with your reading process. Also related to the same issue, is that when referring to the living organisms in this book, I sometimes have used the words "biologically living" which may have the appearance of an unnecessary repetition of the same implications, the Life and the Living. To see why I did this, please refer to Note 1 of Chapter 7.

There are also plenty of italicized words in this book. Italicization has been employed when emphasis on the role and meaning of the *italicized* word is to be relayed.

When there is a need for referring to information given in another chapter, that chapter number is given in parentheses and immediately following the related statement. References to *"NOTES"* are shown as superscript numbers. References to figure credits (where applicable) are shown as superscript numbers at the end of figure legends with the descriptions of the credits cited in the *NOTES* sections at the end of the related chapters. With the exception of Chapters 1 and 14 which have no references, the body of the literature references for each chapter is shown at the end of that chapter.

Introduction

THE MAJOR DIFFERENCE, AND POSSIBLY the most beautiful one, between humans and the rest of the living world is human's ability to think logically and make informed decisions in whatever way he thinks it would suit his interests the best. Under natural circumstances where no external factor is to intervene, and the person enjoys having a sound mind (according to *our* human standards, of course), this ability of making independent decisions is referred to as *"Freewill"*. Since the beginning of the recorded history, generations of *Homo sapiens* have cherished Freewill and have boasted its possession as the sacred line of their separation from lower animals. In almost any culture, literatures have accumulated volumes on the praise of the Freewill and poets have offered their homage to this "heavenly blessing" in the blends of soothingly harmonized clusters of words. Our possession of Freewill has been such a given and obvious an issue that only a very small percentage of humans have ever questioned its existence. "Why I'll definitely go to that movie tonight" or "I am going to the game this weekend" are such common statements in our daily conversations that nothing other than their face values is processed in our brains, neither is registered in our minds. How anything other than what we "freely" choose would be, or could be, possible? When it comes to the *"inside"* of our minds, we believe that we are definitely and infinitely free to decide in whatever way we desire.

Let's review some hypothetical situation: Alice is a 30 years old female with a good job, not married, no children, her parents are still active and independent, has over 30 days of unused vacation and a good bit of surplus cash in her bank account. She loves Europe, is not scared of flying, is not even afraid of traveling alone, and decides she wants to spend two weeks in France and Italy. Of course, it is *her* decision. She can do it so she *will* do it if *she* wants to do it!

But is it? Is the process of her planning, really that simple? Has Alice's decision, about going to France and Italy for two weeks, been made through her own absolute Freewill? Why did she not decide to visit Germany and Switzerland instead? "Because she likes France and Italy better" you may reply. But why? What is *exactly* the reason for her "liking France and Italy better"? "well, maybe she likes French bread and Italian pasta better than Schweinebraten and Zürcher Eintopf, or maybe she prefers Eiffel and Pisa towers to the Brandenburg Gate and the Large Hadron Collider", you reply. Ok, but some "thing" in the depths of the conscious mind is not at ease with your answers. Something having to do with humans' natural curiosity, tickles us back to the same annoying question: "Why?" Why should we prefer one thing over another or make a certain decision rather than a different one? And when we do, is it really a *"Freewill"* anyway?

Questioning these and other seemingly clear and natural daily events and observations may be considered totally irrelevant, unnecessary, and downright even stupid. Who, in his right mind, would question the fundamental existence of the Freewill in Alice's decision-making processes? It looks like it is too obvious a phenomenon that is not even worth the time you spend to pronounce the word "why". But is it? Is the decision-making process, being the product of processes taken place in a natural, material, physical, and 3-dimensional organ called "Brains", not in itself a natural event? And is it not perfectly justified to question, dissect the issue, and at least try to come up with a mechanism through which a natural event takes place, and at the same time, sounds compatible with the physical and scientific knowledge that we have about our World? While such an attempt is not a trivial undertaking, I have tried to share my opinion with you in this book by examining the validity of the Freewill through a *"stepwise logic"* approach. The approach has its foundations on the assumptions that: 1. All matter and energy contents of the universe are related, and 2. All matter and energy contents of the universe have emanated from a starting point known as the Big Bang Singularity. The book's chapters, start out by the citation of a very important principle which I believe we should keep in mind anytime we are evaluating complicated issues. In fact, this principle makes so much sense to me that I decided to allocate the first chapter of this book to it. And then, based on the two reasons just stated, we begin with Chapter 2 which provides a very brief description of the Big Bang theory, followed by a description of the chemical elements (the life's building blocks) in Chapter 3, in an attempt to emphasize on the universal connectivity and relatedness of matter as well as the stepwise pattern of its coming to existence. This "stepwise" pattern is probably one of the strongest evidences to support the universal interconnectivity of all forms of energy and matted, and therefore, all occurring Events. Chapter 4 is devoted to a description of chemical bonds, fateful forces that, in part, hold our Universe together. This chapter also describes molecules, their formation from free atoms, and their role in the creation of the Biosphere. Chapter 5 talks about coming together of molecules to form larger ones, and their importance in the formation and development of the biological life. Chapter 6 describes factors and variables that may play fundamental and direct roles in the formation of molecules and the determining effects that the environmental conditions could have on the type and properties of the product molecules. Chapter 7 touches on the genetic system as a determining factor in the characteristics and behavior of the living organisms followed by Chapter 8 which describes how the properties and functions of any molecule could be related to its structural details. The structure-property issue of Chapter 8 is followed in Chapter 9 where we read about a genetically determined brain structure and its effects on behavior.

As the final message of this book is about Freewill through a proving of Causal (or Physical) Determinism, this latter subject and other related terms are presented in Chapter 10. Two topics, the Chaos and the Quantum theories, which from some points of view may be considered to be antitheses to Determinism, are discussed in Chapters 11 and 12, respectively. I use the word "antitheses" because to some of us, the former theory and at least one interpretation of the latter one, may be indicative of a random and probabilistic nature of the Universe, which in turn, could reject the possibilities of Determinism. So, in addition to some introductory information, I have offered my views on these theories in relation to Determinism, and therefore, to Freewill. Chapter 13 puts together the information from the previous 11 chapters to "synthesize" the "Theory", and finally in Chapter 14 I have tried to clarify the relationship between a deterministic view of the World, the existence of Freewill, and our moral and sociological issues. The rationale behind the writing plan, selection of the topics, and sequential ordering of the chapters of this book, was to demonstrate the universal interconnection that exists among every and all components of this world and how every single Event, no matter how minor or how major they may seem to us, is related to other Events. And it is this chain reaction of Events that started at a singularity of time and space that has been growing with a "Spider Web" pattern. And this pattern is dictated by an evolving logic which had been encrypted within that

Singularity and in the form of an *"Energy-Information Duality"*. I believe no Event is an isolated incidence, and whatever that happens is what was supposed to have happened.

Ahmad Safavy
March, 2017

CHAPTER 1

Occam's Razor[1]

—⚝—

"Pluralitas non est ponenda sine necessitate."

WILLIAM OF OKHAM (OR OCCAM), CA. 1287-1347

English translation:

"Entities should not be multiplied unnecessarily."

Expanded English translation:

"From a set of competing hypotheses, the one with fewest assumptions should be selected."

Notes

[1] In science and philosophy, "razors" are principles used to shave off unlikely explanations for a phenomenon.

CHAPTER 2

The Mother of All Beginnings

—⋘—

"I shall take your mind on a journey. It is a journey of comprehension, taking us to the edge of space, time, and understanding. On it I shall argue that there is nothing that cannot be understood, that there is nothing that cannot be explained, and that everything is extraordinarily simple.."

PETER ATKINS, CHEMISTRY PROFESSOR, OXFORD UNIVERSITY,
IN *CREATION*

THE APPROACH THROUGH WHICH THIS book attempts to arrive at its targeted conclusion is a stepwise one in which the material covered in each chapter has its foundations on the preceding ones. The book, ultimately, is about the World of which we the humans are part of. Since the conclusion, or more specifically, the theory that will be proposed in this book, is based on the structure of our world in its most fundamental sense, I start this chapter with the first chapter of the world's existence, the Big Bang Theory (BBT) (*1*). The BBT is, in my opinion, the most amazing and most clever theories ever proposed by the mankind in the history of its intellectual achievements. Without any intention of being offensive unappreciative to other theories, I reserve and use the "most amazing" and "most clever" adjectives for the BBT because it is a logical and credible explanation of the very beginning of our world. I don't think we could have enjoyed the proposal of another amazing achievement of man, the Quantum Theory, as much, should we have not had any idea about the birth of the world that created that theory in the first place. In my opinion, and maybe in those of many others, being the opening stage of the universal existence, the BBT should be considered *"The Cause"* of any observable (and even unobservable) events taking place in the world at large. And as such, BBT should hold some answers, if not *the* answer, to the questions about our very existence. So, the fortunate and welcome proposition of the Big Bang theory could afford the necessary, though not sufficient, knowledge for being able to answer at least some of our questions. The Sufficient knowledge would be acquired when the "some" in the last sentence becomes "all". This, of course, is something that may not be achievable at the present time, considering our technical limitations. Having acknowledged this though, we could always try to make the best of whatever knowledge we have in finding the answer to our questions. And that's exactly what I shall attempt to do in this book, *try*.

  A standard approach, usually called the scientific method, in solving scientific problems whenever one is encountered through observation, is to propose an appropriate hypothesis which is, to the best of the observer's knowledge capable of fitting the observation, design some experiments based on the proposed hypothesis, gather as much experimental data as possible, and see if the experimental data are compatible with the observation. If they do, a theory could be proposed. To this end, the case of the Universe in which we live (the observation) is not an exception. Based on our knowledge about our intelligence and curiosity, it is expected that *Homo sapiens* has been wondering about, and fascinated with, the secrets of creation from the moment of the beginning of his consciousness. And ignoring the questions about the Creation's fine details, the most fundamental one has been on the *Occurrence* of the material Existence. (Here, I use the adjective "material" to emphasize on the *tangible* world which is capable of being seen and measured, as opposed to the invisible worlds of some schools of superstition which require, even demand, our blind fellowship.) Accordingly, there have been a number of theories trying to answer the question of coming to existence of the Universe, none with more success than the BBT. The success, and the beauty, of this theory is in its ability to explain the observation in a way that is compatible with the currently known scientific principles as well as observational and empirical findings.

The seeds of the BBT were sown for the first time by Georges H.J.E. Lemaitre (1894-1966), a Belgian scientist priest and a professor of physics at the Catholic University of Louvain in Belgium. He was the first to propose in 1927 the Theory of the Expansion of the Universe which is wrongly attributed to Edwin Hubble although Hubble, who was supposedly unaware of Lemaitre's work, reported the Universe's expansion in 1929 while working at the Mt. Wilson Observatory in California (2-4). The theory of the universal expansion stated that all galaxies were moving away from us and from each other in all directions in space. Lemaitre was also the first to propose in 1927 what was later known as the Hubble's Law, and estimated what is now known as the Hubble's Constant, two years before Hubble published his work on the subject and after he made some improvements to Lemaitre's Constant. Lemaitre proposed what became known as the Big Bang theory in his *"Hypothèse de l'Atome Primitif"* (French: *Hypothesis of the Primeval Atom*) (3). Using Hubble's data (4) as a powerful support, Lemaitre's theory proposed that since all heavenly objects, or more specifically galaxies, are moving away from each other, or in other words receding, and since this phenomenon is symmetrical in every direction of space, therefore all of these bodies must have started from the same point of origin which he called the "Primeval Atom".

According to BBT, the Universe, that is, matter, space, and time, was born through a super humongous explosion about 13.7 billion (13.7 thousand, thousand, thousand) years ago. The most mind-boggling part of this theory is that before this event, the Universe we live in today was a tiny spot probably smaller than the tip of a needle (called a Singularity) which was unimaginably hot. I use the word "unimaginable" to describe the temperature, and therefore, the extent of energy density of the Singularity because it really *is* hard to imagine that such humongous amount of energy, which only part of it turned into all the matter we see today such as the planets, the stars, the galaxies, and the clusters of the galaxies, was all concentrated and contained in one tiny spot.[1] The question about the age of this singularity, that is, how old this spot was before it exploded is, by the way, irrelevant because the time itself did not exist until it was created *with* the Big Bang. Before the big B, there *was* no time (see below).

When we are presented with such a description, it is only natural to picture a completely empty, physically infinite and dark space in which this enormous explosion takes place and suddenly there is a universe. Although this picture by itself is already wonderful enough, it is not what happened, at least according to the current conclusions of scientists. The results of the painstaking research of these incredibly smart and talented people tell us that our picture of the BB just described was only 50% correct: Yes, we did have a huge explosion which initiated the formation of the material Universe as well as Time; what we did *not* have, though, was a completely empty, physically infinite, and dark space! We did not have a space, period, because space, also, was created *with* and *through* the Big Bang. In fact, it is irrelevant to think of the BB as an explosion that started at a certain point. And here, by "point" I mean a physical spot somewhere in a space, because there *was* no space as absolute "nothingness" ruled. Think of the BB as an unthinkably rapid expansion of the surface, and therefore volume, of an infinitesimally small balloon. Our balloon, however, did not have a skin. That is, the contents were not enclosed in, say a membrane, or any type of enclosing material for that matter. As a result of this rapid expansion, space and time came into existence with the release of an enormous amount of energy that, in part, was converted to matter. In fact, from the vantage point of a hypothetical observer, the Big Bang might have been viewed as a "now-you-don't-see-it-now-you-do" event. Just for the sake of the discussion, try to picture an imaginary person standing 13.7 billion years ago somewhere (doesn't matter where because there *was* no "where") witnessing the BB explosion. If the person was lucky enough to survive the explosion, he would see that he was suddenly surrounded by the World in such a way that there was near-perfect symmetry in the surroundings and in every direction of that newly formed universe.

Although an in-depth discussion of the BBT is out of the scope of this book, it may be helpful (especially to those still in doubt) to mention that the theory is supported by some solid evidences. The main evidence was the phenomenon of the receding galaxies noted by Georges Lemaitre which was mentioned above (2). There are two more firm evidences in support of the BBT which I would like to mention here, namely, the Cosmic Microwave Background (CMB) radiation and the universal hydrogen-to-helium ratio.

The existence of the CMB radiation was first predicted in 1948 by Ralph Alpher (1921-2007) and Robert Herman (1914-1997) (5), followed by its first "published recognition" in 1964 by Andrei Doroshkevich (1937) and Igor Novikov (1935). Although a number of scientists and research groups worked on the subject, the actual measurement and physical proof of CMB radiation was demonstrated by Arno Penzias (1933) and Robert Wilson (1936) in 1965 and at the

Bell Telephone Laboratories in New Jersey (5). They shared the Nobel Prize in physics in 1978 for their work on the CMB radiation.

Presuming that the meanings of the words "cosmic", "background", and "radiation" are pretty much clear to the readers of this book, I shall only briefly discuss the remaining one, "microwave", in here. As far as our human senses, knowledge, and instrumentation could tell us, energy in its radiation form, is defined by a wavelength-frequency continuum called the electromagnetic spectrum. All the colors and lights visible to the human eye are part of this spectrum, although there are other parts that are not visible to us but they may be to some other animals. Some fish, for example, could see light at wavelengths longer than we could see. On the other hand, shorter wavelengths, such as some bands of the ultraviolet light which are invisible to humans, are readily picked up by birds, butterflies, and bees.

The long- and the short-wavelength extremes of the electromagnetic spectrum consist of the low-energy and high-energy radiations, respectively. Each given point on the continuum is defined by a discrete frequency (usually measured in Hertz, Hz) and a discrete wavelength (usually measured in nanometers, nm, or micrometers, µm). The radiation energy is directly proportional to its frequency but inversely proportional to its wavelength. In other words, the higher the frequency of a radiation, the higher its energy but the longer its wavelength, and *vice versa*. Microwave radiation is part of the electromagnetic spectrum which is categorized as a (relatively) low-energy radiation with thermal (heat-generating) properties and is located in the low-frequency (long wavelength) region of the electromagnetic spectrum. It also falls into a region of spectrum which is not visible to the human eye.

When looked at through a regular optical telescope, the interstellar and intergalactic space looks completely dark and completely empty. However, using a heat-sensitive (or infrared) telescope, however, reveals the existence of a weak thermal radiation which fills all the space uniformly and in all directions. The intensity of this radiation is maximal in the microwave region of the electromagnetic spectrum, and interestingly, it is not associated with, that is, not irradiated by, any star, galaxy, or any other cosmological body. The intensity of the CMB glow is nearly uniform in all directions of space but there are still very minute energy variations called anisotropies or irregularities. These irregularities in the CMB radiation have been examined and measured very carefully and have revealed an absolutely amazing secret: The irregular regions of the CMB radiation fit the characteristics of what would have happened if small thermal variations of an extremely tiny space had expanded to the present size of today's Universe. Since, as mentioned above, CMB radiation could not be associated with any cosmological body, and at the same time its presence has to be explained by some model, it has been concluded that this detected CMB is the remnant radiation of the energy released by the Big Bang explosion. In other words, the Big Bang and CMB mutually justify and prove each other. No physical model other than the Big Bang has ever been able to explain the existence of the CMB radiation. In fact, when calculated on the basis of a Big Bang model, the theoretically calculated intensities of the remnant radiations of such an explosion *exactly* matched the real-time intensities picked up by NASA's Cosmic Background Explorer (COBE) satellite.

So now let's take a look at the other evidential support for the BBT, the hydrogen-to-helium ratio. At this time and age, all of us know that the material world is made of atoms. The classical (but not necessarily the most perfect) definition of an atom is "the smallest fraction of matter which cannot be further divided (Latin: ἄτομος, *atomos*, indivisible). Just for the sake of the discussion and hoping not to get too technical here, let's go one step further and define an atom as the combination of a central nucleus and one or more electrons. Until we start the next chapter, where you will find definitions for the atomic nuclei, nuclear contents, and electrons, this is all we need to know so I could tell you that the simplest atom in nature is hydrogen, a gaseous substance which has one nucleus and only one electron. In the two-dimensional space of our textbook pages we illustrate the hydrogen atom as a small circle (the nucleus) in the middle of a larger circle as the orbit (or the path) of the circling electron. A more realistic picture would be a three-dimensional space where, instead of flat circles, we have a small sphere surrounded by a larger one to represent the nucleus and the electron's orbital, respectively. Just imagine one tiny round shot, as tiny as one grain of beach sand, happily suspended inside and in the center of a beach ball as large as a football field. That's roughly the proportion of the distance from the hydrogen atom's nucleus (the tiny shot) to the orbital path of the hovering electron (the surface of the beach ball). By "the orbital path of the electron" I mean the surface of the sphere that the electron is confined to hover by travelling at extremely high speeds. These discussions will be reviewed in more detail in Chapter 3.

The second simplest atom is helium, consisting of one nucleus and two electrons. Helium was made from hydrogen by a nuclear fusion reaction called *nucleosynthesis*, within the first 3 minutes after the start of the BB. Although trace amounts of both hydrogen and helium are still being made through stellar core processes, the main quantities of these two elements were produced by the BB. Now let's see how these two tiny atoms give solid support to the validity of the BBT: Through mathematical calculations, the Big Bang Theory predicts that the ratio of the number of all hydrogen atoms to helium atoms should be 10. That is, for each helium atom found in the cosmos, there have to be ten hydrogen atoms. That's exactly what has been found through experimental observations and there is no part of the universe where this ratio has been found to be breached (6). Usually in scientific research, when the experimental values match the theoretical ones, it could be safely concluded that the hypothesized model is valid. By the same procedure, the observed and calculated hydrogen-to-helium ratios, coupled to their mechanism of formation, support the Big Bang theory.

Since BBT is of core importance to the subject issue of this book, it may be a good idea to also mention its now-discredited principal rival, the Steady State Theory (SST) (7). This model was proposed in 1948 by cosmologists Thomas Gold (1920-2004) and Hermann Bondi (1919-2005), and was immediately adopted by their famous collaborator, the astrophysicist Fred Hoyle (1915-2001). The main drive behind the suggestion of SST was proposing an alternative to Lemaitre's Big Bang Theory to which these scientists were opposed. According to the SST, matter is continuously generated as the Universe expands in such a way that there is no change in the overall shape of the Universe (thus the term "Steady State"), and therefore, it has no beginning and no end. Although there were a number of observations that contributed to the demise of the SST, the "final nail in the coffin of the Steady State Theory", as the theoretical physicist Stephen Hawking (1942) put it, came from the discovery of the CMB radiation discussed above. In addition to the CMB radiation evidence, there are more recent progress in establishing further scientific supports. These have come about as recently as the late 1990s and early this century through the advances in telescope technology as well as the analyses of satellite data gathered by the COBE, the Hubble Space Telescope, and WMAP (Wilkinson Microwave Anisotropy Probe). These instruments allow scientists to look deep into space and see galaxies in the conditions they were in billions of years ago. This is possible because, due to their extremely far distances from us, it takes their light billions of years to reach us. So, looking at that light is like you are looking at an event as it was taking place billions of years ago. This procedure is called "looking back in time". By looking back in time, scientists have found out that, unlike what the SST proposes, the Universe has actually undergone significant changes since its formation and this gives another firm support for the Big Bang and against the SST.

So, unless we wake up one day and there is a better explanation of the creation of our world, which is also supported by solid experimental evidence, the BBT is by far the most logical and evidence-compatible explanation of the coming into existence of the cosmos which includes the space, time, matter, and therefore, plants, animals, and yes, humans.

It is also interesting to note that the term *"Big Bang"* was coined for the first time by one of its opponents, Dr. Fred Hoyle himself during a BBC radio broadcast in March of 1949 when he referred to Lemaitre's explosive origin of the Universe as ".. this big bang idea .."

Well, now that we have some clues as to how this universe got started to *be*, let's flip the page on to the next chapter to see how the *components* of this tangible world of ours came to existence.

NOTES

[1] The energy that was converted to matter was only part of the total amount of the original energy. The rest of it constitutes the remaining, "immaterialized" energy still present in nature, as well as dark matter and dark energy which are discussed in Chapter 3.

REFERENCES

1. Silk, Joseph. A Short History of the Universe. *Scientific American Library*, New York, 1994.
2. Lemaitre G, Un Univers Homogene de Masse Constant et de Rayon Croissant Compte de la Radiale des Nebuleuses Extra-Galactiques, *Ann de la Soc Sci de Bruxelles*, A, 47: 49–56, 1927.
3. Kragh H, The Beginning of the World: Georges Lemaitre and the Expanding Universe, *Centaurus*, 30 (2): 114-139, 1987.
4. Hubble EP, A Relation between Distance and Radial Velocity among Extra-Galactic Nebulae, *Proc. Natl Acad Sci USA*, 15: 168-173, 1929.
5. Penzias AA, Wilson RW, A Measurement of Antenna Temperature at 4080 Mc/s, *Astrophys J*, 142 (1): 419-421, 1965.
6. Beatty JJ, The isotopes of hydrogen and helium in the Galactic cosmic radiation - Their source abundances and interstellar propagation, *Astrophys J* (Part 1), 311: 425-436, 1986.
7. Hoyle F, A New Model for the Expanding Universe, *MNRAS*, 108: 172, 1948.

CHAPTER 3

The Building Blocks of our Tangible World

—⁂—

THERE ARE MANY DIFFERENT WAYS of classifying the contents of our cosmos. One of the most general and all-inclusive ones may by dividing them into two main classes of visible and invisible. Although the word "invisible" may give you an impression of superstition, fantasy, and science fiction, there really is invisible stuff in the universe, at least according to our current data-backed scientific information. The easiest-to-realize invisible elements in nature are sound waves as well as the part of electromagnetic radiation that is out of the range of frequencies detectable by the human eye. Nobody has ever *seen* the sounds of Mozart's *symphony number 25 in G minor* or Queen's *Bohemian Rhapsody*. The absolute joy that the fans of these musicians' experience would be through their ears and by the sound perception and processing systems in their brains. By the same token, no patient has ever directly and visually witnessed the passage of the X-rays through their bodies that reveal the site of the damage to their bones. Neither could the attending radiologist, with years of training in medical school and residency. It is the *effect* of those naughty rays on the photographic film or computer monitor screen which is visible to both the doctor and the patient.

There are more members in the group of the invisibles. The next class is a bit more complicated, mysterious, and by all means dark. And although this one truly sounds like science fiction, to the best of calculations of top-notch astrophysicists, it may very possibly be a reality. The names of the members of this invisible duo are Dark Matter and Dark Energy (1). Dark matter's existence was proposed after discrepancies were noticed between the calculated mass of the large cosmological objects, such as galaxies and their clusters, and those of the visible bodies they contain (that are, stars, interstellar dust, *etc.*). Based on all of these studies it was suggested that dark matter forms 82% of the whole material content of the Universe at large, and therefore, all that we can see anywhere is only 18% of the totality of the universe's matter! In other words, there is more invisible dark matter in this world than visible matter. By definition an "invisible" object, or dark matter in this case, is one that neither emits nor absorbs electromagnetic radiation including visible light. To clarify, let's say you have a football sitting in the corner of your room. If that ball is reflecting the visible light (like sunlight or the light coming from a lightbulb) then you will see the football as it is. But if it does not reflect the light, all you could see would be an oval-shaped black stuff in the corner of your room (which could be really spooky if you didn't know what it was).

The existence of dark energy was hypothesized on the observation that the Universe was expanding at a mysterious acceleration. "Acceleration" means an increase in the speed of a moving object with respect to time. Based on calculations and circumstantial evidence it has been suggested that dark energy is a weak but homogeneous power that fills all the otherwise empty parts of space. Without going into much detail about the dark side, let's suffice by saying that the total energy-mass content of the Universe has been proposed to be about 74% dark energy, 22% dark matter, and 4% ordinary matter. That is, all the matter in the Universe that could be seen and/or touched (or is capable of being seen and/or being touched) constitutes only 4% of the grand total amounts of energy plus matter in the Universe. Yes, it is an amazing world! And more amazing is the fact that the more we discover it, the more complicated it gets. An absolutely endless but full-of-excitement tunnel.

Now let's come back to the more familiar part of cosmos, the one that we could see and touch. This class falls into two master categories of Light and Matter. Although the entire range of the electromagnetic spectrum in its nature is light of different frequencies, let's focus here just on the part that's more familiar to us, the visible light. Without much need for introduction, it is one of the most beautiful elements of Nature's creation that shows us the world throughout our lives. And it is a phenomenon in response to which nature has created one of its most mind-boggling miracles: The Eye!

When we see an object, we are really seeing the reflection of the visible light off of that object and could know that the object is really there, and most of the time, what it is. The "visible" region of the electromagnetic spectrum includes light in the wavelength range of 400-700 nanometers (nm). And why all those colors? Colors have to do with the different wavelengths in the visible light and the chemical structure of any given object which reflects one or a combination of wavelengths from the visible region of the electromagnetic spectrum. For example, yellow is light with a wavelength of about 580 nm and blue is around 460-495 nm, whereas the color green is a combination of these two. Visible light at any wavelength is picked up by the eye, changed into an electrical signal which is then sent to the brain where it is translated into the real-world information to tell us what it is that we are looking at. But with all its beauty, significance to life, and its importance even to the point of sacredness, we are not going to spend more time on Light as our focus need be on the next component of the visible universe: Matter.

The Atomic Structure

Generally speaking, "Matter" is whatever the visible and tangible world is made of and which is composed of atoms. This is a simplistic definition of matter without going into the discussion of the elementary particles that constitute atoms. Our simple definition, though, holds regardless of the different physical states of matter that are solids, liquids, and gases. As mentioned in the last chapter, atoms are classically defined as the smallest division of matter, although this may not be the most perfect description of them. The reason is that by now, we know the atom itself is composed of several different types of elementary (or subatomic) particles. I will briefly touch on these particles later in this chapter but for right now let's look at the atomic structure at the nucleic and electronic levels, or the structure formed by the particles I would like to call the *"Second Generation"* particles for reasons we will discuss later.

Structurally, an atom consists of a central nucleus surrounded by one (in the case of hydrogen) or more (in the case of higher atoms) electrons which revolve around the nucleus at super-high speeds and in dimensionally well-defined areas of space called orbitals. In simple language, orbitals (first termed as such by the Nobel laureate chemist Robert S. Mulliken, 1896-1986) are the part of space around the atomic nucleus where the probability of finding electrons exists. The physical values for this "probability" are calculated by a mathematical relationship called the Schrödinger equation, after the Austrian Nobel laureate physicist Erwin Schrödinger (1887-1961) (2). The totality of these orbitals and their electronic content is called "the electronic cloud". In atoms higher than hydrogen and helium, these orbitals are organized next to one another in an amazingly complicated but ordered fashion. The net result is formation of atoms that if you could see them individually in free form, would look like well-defined spheres. If you remember the beach ball example for hydrogen atom which was described in the last chapter, the body of the ball, the thin plastic membrane that holds the air inside, is the orbital in which the single electron of the hydrogen atom orbits around the central nucleus. In order to generate a "beach ball" model of higher atoms, you will need many additional, not only beach balls, but pear-shaped and doughnut-shaped balloons (to represent other forms of orbitals) all interlocked into one another, and layer by layer like an onion and according to their energy levels. As a whole, an atom may be considered to be a spherically shaped system. Hopefully, for following the issues discussed in this book we will be able to get by just with the information given so far and without worrying too much about the fine-structural and topological details of these complicated and tiny, yet wondrous, orbital systems.

The atomic nucleus, on the other hand, comes only in one compound piece, albeit a very heavy one when compared to electrons. The atomic nuclei consist of protons and neutrons densely packed together in the center of the atom. Compared to the overall size of the atom, nuclei occupy only a small volume. The major part of the bulk of an atom is the space or the unoccupied distances between the nuclei and their orbiting electrons as well as the inter-electronic space. Compared to an electron (e), a proton (p) enjoys a much heavier weight with a p-to-e mass ratio of about 1,836. This means you need 1,836 electrons to balance off the mass of one single proton. Neutrons have a slightly higher mass than protons. Therefore, the major portion of the weight of any objet, including the human body, comes from the *nuclei* of its constituent atoms. This reminds me of a poster on my office wall a few years ago which suggested to the reader *"Be humble! 75% of you is water and the rest is just empty space between electrons."*

The fact that *all* atoms are composed of nuclei (protons plus neutrons) and electrons, leads to a very important conclusion: Having the atom of hydrogen at hand, all other atoms may be constructed from it by just adding, well ... not water, but protons and neutrons to the nuclei and electrons to their corresponding orbitals. And let me tell you that it's not something you could do in your kitchen or garage but it *is* doable and both Nature, and to some far lesser extent humans, have done it with great success as we shall see in the following section.

The Periodic Table Of Chemical Elements

If sometime in the future, somebody from another galaxy and another civilization visited Earth and wanted to rank the greatest achievements of the *Homo sapiens* species, the Periodic Table of the Chemical Elements should occupy a very high place. In my opinion, it even deserves a high place in both science *and* art rankings as it implies some artful putting together of this fundamental puzzle of Nature. In addition to showing the systematic way that atoms are ordered in nature, the Periodic Table is a visualization of the "periodic" relationship which exists among them. The first mental sparks in chemists' minds jumped by the observation that elements with the same number of valence electrons showed similar properties. More than one chemist noticed these atomic relationships, and thus, could contribute to the discovery of the Table. While the first formal version of it was published by chemist Dmitri Mendeleev in 1869 (3), the German chemist Julius Lothar von Meyer (1830-1895) independently published his version of the Table in 1870. The major credit, however, went to Mendeleev so the Periodic Table is also known as the Mendeleev Table.

Now let's take a little closer look at this important tool: Those of us who have taken science courses, especially chemistry, in high school or college have probably seen this sizable tableau that depicted a rather complicated grid format containing a bunch of letters and numbers in its squares (or cells). It may also be remembered that the table was divided into several sections each with a different color. To be fair, I should say that, at least in the first glance, the thing is sort of intimidating but it may get friendlier once we learn a little bit more about its secrets. To that end, let's first find out what "chemical elements" really are: A chemical element is any substance that is made of only one kind of atom, a condition for which I would like to propose the term *"homoatomic"*. All the elements known to date come in three different physical forms: Gas (such as hydrogen, helium, and oxygen), liquid (bromine, mercury), and solid (sulfur, calcium, iron). Chemical elements are the building blocks of everything in the material universe including stars, planets, mountains, oceans, plants, animals, and humans. At the time of this writing, there are 118 reported chemical elements the first of which is hydrogen and the last oganesson (chemical symbol "*Og*"). The element Og was made by a group of American and Russian scientists in 2002 and was formally named in 28th of November, 2016 (*4, 5*).

In the Periodic Table, elements are organized in 7 rows (top to bottom) and 18 columns (left to right) with respect to their atomic numbers. An *"atomic number"* is the number of protons contained in the nucleus of an atom. By contrast, *"mass number"* is the sum of the number of protons plus the number of neutrons, the latter also being contained in an atom's nucleus. Mass number is the major contributor to the real (physical) weight of an atom, and therefore, of any substance. A question you might ask now is, if electrons are another component of atoms, what about them? Why are *they* excluded from the weight calculation? The answer is that the electrons' contribution to the overall weight of atoms is negligibly small due to their very light weight. As described in the previous section, the mass of an electron is 1,836 times smaller than that of a proton. The mass of a neutron is just slightly more than that of a proton. Therefore, whereas each proton-neutron pair contributes 2 mass units to the overall mass of an atom, an electron's contribution to that mass would be only $1/1836 = 0.00054$ units, and therefore, negligible. The names of the elements in the Periodic Table are represented as abbreviations, called "chemical symbols", using one or two alphabetical letters. The single-letter abbreviation, or the first letter of the two-letter abbreviation, is capitalized while the second one (if any) would be in lower case. For example, hydrogen is shown as H and calcium as Ca. Adding to the information are two numbers shown on the lower and upper left corners of the abbreviation letters, showing the atomic number and the mass number of the element, respectively. So, for our exemplary elements you will see the following notations in a Periodic Table:

$_{1}^{1}H$ $\quad\quad\quad$ $_{20}^{40}Ca$
Hydrogen $\quad\quad$ Calcium

Another question which you may ask is why in the world do we call this a *"periodic"* table? This is, of course a valid question the answer to which reveals one of the amazing ways that Nature has put things together in a systematic manner to create the material part of the world we live in.

Some of us (and I emphasize *some*, not all) look at the world and its creation as a random and chaotic phenomenon. And this may be true even of those who already believe in science and have every intention to look at the world through a purely scientific view and build their beliefs squarely on solid scientific foundations. According to this school of thought, after their creation through whatever means and mechanism, atoms came together randomly, to make molecules and molecules randomly aggregated to form organisms. The better, *more adaptive*, organisms survived the natural reactionary forces (which themselves were randomly generated) and produced the next *better* and more adaptable generation of organisms. This process, about which volumes have been written throughout our history, went on and on to produce the world and its contents as we see them today. According to that particular view, every step was random, and therefore, all the products (*i.e.*, objects, plants, animals, *etc.*), were randomly assembled! While I could agree with a major part of this theory, I have some difficulty with the "random" aspect of it. But we shall examine this theory in more detail later and towards the end of the book, but for right now, let's take a look at one of the most fundamental steps taken by the Nature to form our Universe, that is, the creation of atoms, the building blocks of the tangible world.

The visible and touchable world is made of atoms so atoms are a real and undeniable fact. Therefore, learning about the properties of these building units would be very helpful in dissecting some "worldly issues" as we shall do later in this book. To go through this learning process, even as a non-scientist reader, it is essential to take a brief look at the Periodic Table of the Elements. The collective information provided by this valuable source would be one of the main tools to hopefully lead us to the conclusion I am intending to arrive at by the end of this book.

Let's return to our question "why the Table is called Periodic?" As mentioned in the last paragraph, there are 7 rows in the Table. Mendeleev and some other clever chemists had noticed that some chemical and physical properties of certain elements recurred periodically after each 7 set of the elements. In fact, a good part of Mendeleev's own reputation was because of his ability to predict the properties of the *missing* elements of the Table. By "missing" I mean the elements which had not yet been discovered at the time of the initial organization of the table. The "prediction" process went as follows: If the periodicity principle was real and element A had some certain characteristics, then element B, which was the eighth element after A (counting from left to right), should have properties very similar to A. This, in turn, could lead to the conclusion that the still-missing element C, the sixteenth element from A and eighth one from B, had to have the same kind of properties and that space was reserved for it. If a newly discovered element showed those characteristics it could be readily placed into that reserved Table position for element C, and was assigned an appropriate name and abbreviation. Based on this observed periodicity, Mendeleev was able to make predictions about the yet-undiscovered elements which later turned out to be true. Based on these periodically recurring properties of each set of the elements, the rows were called "periods", and naturally, the table was called "The Periodic Table of the Elements".

The reason I included the Periodic Table in this chapter was to demonstrate how Nature has made its building blocks, the atoms, in an absolutely orderly fashion. While the Table nicely shows such an order by revealing how all chemical elements are related to one another (what I may call an *"inter-elemental"* order), it does not say much about a second type of "order" that Nature imposes on each individual atomic structure. This order, which is just as important as the inter-elemental order, demonstrates the discrete rules which each subatomic particle has to follow before a single atom of any individual chemical element could be born. These rules are the subject of the following sections.

How To Build Atoms

Ignoring its sub-nuclear features, and despite their increasingly complicated structures (as they get bigger), the principle of making atoms is pretty straightforward: Atoms are nothing but aggregations of nucleons (or the contents of the nuclei, that are, protons and neutrons) with electrons. The only caveat is that there is an absolute need for gigantic amounts of energy to assemble all parts to build an atom. This energy requirement makes Nature, and Nature only, the single proprietor of the art of large-scale manufacturing of stable atoms, a process called *Nucleosynthesis*. At small scales, however, humans have been able to synthesize atoms with limited stability in the laboratory. The combination word "nucleosynthesis" refers to the process of "making" (-synthesis) of atomic nuclei (nucleo-). In this process, protons and neutrons are bound together by a force called *Strong Nuclear Force* to form the atomic nuclei to which are added electrons to complete the "creation". More of this later in this chapter when we talk about elementary particles.

Now since the idea behind citing all these discussions in this chapter is to show the "ordered" manner by which the Universe has made itself, let's go all the way to the fundamental aspects of the formation of atoms. First, let us find out how we, our family members, our pets, our homes, cars, foods, and the rest of the world around us, are held together. Did we not say everything was made of atoms and atoms themselves are made of other tinier stuff? So why when I look into the mirror I see *me*, and looking around, I see my family, my house, my car, my pet and everything else? Well, the master sculptor Nature has many tools in her box to shape the world, including forces which she puts to use as *"glues"* for sticking things together. There are four types of forces operating in Nature: Electromagnetism, gravity, the weak nuclear force, and the strong nuclear force. The electromagnetism is the force operating among electrically charged particles. It consists of the two words *elektron* (Greek: amber, as the electrostatic phenomenon was supposedly first noticed in this natural substance by the philosopher Thales[1]) and *magnets*, the property of magnetic stones found in Lydia, Asia Minor, once part of the Greater Persian Empire. As a universal rule, a positively charged system is attracted to a negatively charged one (and *vice versa*) through this kind of interaction. Electromagnetic interaction is particularly important in the case of ionized atoms and molecules, those carrying positive or negative electric charges due to loss or gain of electrons, respectively. Because electrons carry negative charges, atoms or molecules undergoing electron loss become positively charged and are referred to as cations. Conversely, those gaining electrons turn into negatively charged species called anions. The ionization process plays an important role in nature especially in physiological processes.

    The next force, gravity, probably needs no introduction as we all use it to happily live and walk on our beloved planet Earth. It is also the force that brought the proverbial apple down to spark the "Aha!" moment of Isaac Newton. It is important to remember though that gravity is not limited only to Earth. It operates among any and all masses of matter and is the major force that holds all the heavenly objects suspended in space with their amazingly harmonious arrangements. According to the laws governing this force, anything with mass will attract anything else with mass. In extreme cases, there even is no need for both sides to have mass: Black holes, the huge masses of collapsed stars shrunk to extremely small volumes, have such a huge force of gravity that even light, which has no mass, cannot escape them when getting too close to them. In another example, the beams of light from certain stars are "bent" when passing through supermassive stars and black holes vicinities. This latter phenomenon, called *"gravitational lensing"*, had been predicted theoretically by Albert Einstein (1879-1955) in his work on General Relativity (6).

The third force, the weak nuclear force (or the weak interaction), is responsible for the decay of radioactive nuclei and the hydrogen fusion reaction in stars such as our Sun. The hydrogen fusion reaction is the source of Sun's energy (in the form of light and heat) which has brought about life on our planet. Ironically, if some theories turn out to be correct, the very same energy may someday terminate life on this planet as the Sun will gradually get too hot for the terrestrial water to stay in a liquid form (7). The good news, however, is that it will be roughly another 5 billion years before that happens.

Finally, the strong nuclear force (or simply the strong force) is the force responsible for holding the nucleons (protons and neutrons) together. When we use the word "nucleus", it may relay a mental picture in which the nuclear contents are confined within a membrane or some other sort of container. This is not the case for the atomic nuclei though. The nucleons are held together by the strong force without the help from any type of "container". Atomic nucleus carries a positive charge from the protons as neutrons have no electrical charge (thereby the name neutron).

Well, now that we have an idea about the *"cosmic glues"* let's go back to the "material" part of atoms, the component particles that these glues hold together. It was mentioned earlier that the main focus of this book, on the way to arriving at its targeted final conclusion, was to show the systematic and highly ordered manner in which the material universe is built. I use the words *"material universe"* because everything, ourselves included, is part of this universe. In this quest, therefore, focusing on the structure of atoms as a starting point is unavoidable. Still, compared to the depth of the available knowledge on atomic structure and components, I am really touching the very surface of the subject in this book and just enough to get by with building the idea needed to catch the point of this whole discussion. Nevertheless, I do not believe the relay of this information would be done right if I did not mention something about other yet more fundamental components of an atom than protons, neutrons, and electrons. These fundamental components are called *Elementary Particles*, which by definition, are particles with no substructure, and as such, are not made of smaller components. In my personal classification, I call these the *"First Generation"* particles as opposed to protons, neutrons, and electrons which I put in my *"Second Generation"* particle category. As of the writing of this book, these are the end points in the structural dissection of our material universe although I am not sure if there is still more in the farther depths of the "atomic abyss". So, let's take a look at them:

According to particle physics, the part of science that deals with these mysterious and by all means extremely tiny beings, there are two types of elementary particles (EPs): Fermions and Bosons (*8*). Fermions, named after the theoretical and experimental physicist, Enrico Fermi (1901-1954), are characterized by Fermi-Dirac statistics, a part of physics that deals with particles' energies. Bosons are governed by the Bose-Einstein statistics, also a branch of physics dealing with particles' energies, and named after physicist Satyendra Nath Bose (1894-1974). A very interesting outcome of these studies was that fermions are associated with matter while bosons are related to the fundamental forces mentioned above, electromagnetism, gravity, and the weak and the strong nuclear forces. We will leave bosons right here to keep things a touch simpler but do need to take one further step with the fermions since they relate, materially, to the atomic structure. In our diving expedition into the abyss of matter, we started with atom, noted the speedy orbiting of its electrons, then into its nuclear protons and neutrons which are held together by the strong force, and down to fermions, and now we discovered that the abyss has not bottomed out yet! Let's take a deep breath and continue the dive one step farther: Quantum mechanical studies in particle physics have shown that fermions themselves are branched into two groups of elementary particles, *quarks* and *leptons*. Quarks are elementary particles responsible for forming Matter. There are six different types (or as physicists call them, "*flavors*") of quarks so far discovered in particle physics: Up, Down, Strange, Charm, Top, and Bottom. The last four flavors are heavier in mass and are unstable, decaying into the Up and Down quarks. The Up and Down quarks are combined in different proportions to form *Hadrons*. The most stable forms of hadrons are protons and neutrons, the components of atomic nuclei. Thus, two Up and one Down quark combine to make a proton while combination of one Up and two Down quarks forms neutrons. And that's how quarks, and therefore fermions, are the foundations of all forms of Matter in the Universe.

Alright, so much for quarks but what about the other kind of fermions mentioned a few lines earlier, the leptons? To be fair, Nature gave leptons an assignment too: For the atoms to be born, leptons came into play to form electrons, the very particles responsible for two important features of matter: 1. Charge neutrality (to balance off the proton's positive charge), and 2. Chemical property (or chemical character, an extremely important feature as we shall see later in the later chapters of this book). It should be easy to appreciate that a world with only positively charged atomic nuclei could not be a stable, and therefore, a livable world. An exclusively positively (or negatively) charged universe would be a chaotic one in which no chemical bonds, therefore no molecules (water, oxygen, proteins, genes, animals, humans, *etc.*), and thus no life, could commence. The reason is simply the repelling each other of the like electrical charges as well as destructive interactions of the particles with cosmic rays. Just like when you bring the north pole of a magnet to the north pole of another and they push each other away, the approach of a positively (or negatively) charged particle to another positively (or negatively) charged one will cause a repelling reaction.

It should be easy to see then, that formation of any kind of chemical bond (which is a necessary condition for the development of the World in general and the biological life in particular) in a homogeneously charged world would be impossible. No attractions, no bonds, thus no Life!

The second role played by electrons, the induction of chemical properties including chemical reactivity, is just as important as the first one. In a simple language, *chemical reactivity* means the "ease" at which an atom (or molecule) makes bonds to one or more other atoms (or molecules). In the case of molecules, the term may also refer to the ease of self-disintegration into new species, either all the way back to the constituting atoms, or to smaller molecules, or both.

There are two major classes of chemical bonds in nature: Covalent and ionic (discussed in Chapter 4). In both cases, electrons play the key role. In covalent bonding, an electron from one reactant (either an atom or a molecule) shares one or more of its electrons with the electron(s) of another atom or molecule. Simply put, two atoms or molecules "share" their valence electrons (VEs, defined below). Covalent bonds are electrically neutral. The driving force behind formation of a covalent bond is achieving chemical stability through this sharing of electrons.

Now, we should be able to appreciate how extremely important, not only the compact and positively charged atomic nuclei, but also the tiny, light, speedy, and negatively charged electrons are in forming our world, and therefore, our lives.

Just for the sake of completing this section, I should say something about the other type of lepton. There are two types of leptons, charged and neutral. The charged type is our just-mentioned electron with one negative electrical charge. The neutral lepton is called *Neutrino* which means *"the tiny neutral one"* in Italian (9). Even on the scale of subatomic particles, neutrinos are considered tiny. In fact, so much so that although we know neutrinos have a mass, that mass has never been measured accurately (Arthur B. McDonald (1943) and Takaaki Kajita (1959) shared the 2015 Nobel Prize for the discovery that neutrinos do have mass). Neutrinos are generated by some types of radioactive decay, as well as through collision of cosmic rays with atoms, by nuclear processes in nuclear reactors, and in nuclear reactions such as those occurring in our Sun. Furthermore, in contrast to electrons with their "gregarious" character (as evidenced by their induction of chemical reactivity in atoms and molecules), neutrinos are solitaries and do not interact with normal matter. About 65 billion solar neutrinos per second pass through each square centimeter of our planet which is perpendicularly exposed to sunrays. As with everything else, neutrinos do not interact with our discussion here either, since they are not a component of the atomic structure. Let's then just suffice with these few introductory lines about them and move on to the next very interesting section.

THE AUFBAU PRINCIPLE

Along the way of showing the ordered manner in which our world is made, and to that end following the description of the atomic structure, I think it is only appropriate to touch on another scientific discovery. This is just one more piece of evidence pointing to the orderly way in which the World is made and to how Nature works according to a well-defined logic. This scientific discovery is now known as the *"Aufbau Principle"* (German: *aufbau*, construction) but before starting to talk about this principle let me define for you some other rules and principles as they may help to get a better grasp of the aufbau subject. These definitions are, of course, significantly simplified to be useful to everybody. All that is needed would be simply developing a feel for the point of discussion. Even if these definitions are not clear at this point, the purpose of introducing them here will be readily touchable when we get a little bit farther down into the section. So here we go:

Spin (in the context of particles physics) – Spin is an intrinsic property of some elementary particles and atomic nuclei related to the rotational situation of a given particle such as an electron or a nucleus. It could have either a negative or a positive quantized (or discrete) value. To fully occupy an atomic orbital, one electron of each spin sign pairs up with its counterpart (like a +1/2 with a -1/2 spin) to yield an overall zero spin for the occupied orbital.

Pauli Exclusion Principle (PEP) – Named after the Austrian-Swiss physicist, Wolfgang Pauli (1900-1958), this principle requires that no two similar fermions (for example electrons) could occupy the same quantum state *(10)*. Now let's translate this into plain English. We may remember from our earlier discussions that both electrons and atomic nuclei belong to the fermion group of elementary particles. Saving a good bit of quantum mechanics jargon, PEP basically alerts that it is not possible, even for the Nature herself, to keep two elementary particles with the same spin, in the same box! And yes, the word "box" in here is totally hypothetical and is used strictly for the elucidation of the point of the discussion. To physically exemplify this rule, we may think of attempting to bring the north poles of two small pieces of magnet really close to each other. Just picture it in your mind and you'll readily feel that you have to make an effort to do this as the two pieces tend to repel each other. Since you are physically much stronger than the two humble little pieces of magnets, of course, you will definitely be able to put them as close as you want. But here is the point: That "effort" that you have to make to do this, and that of Nature's to put two like-spin particles in the same state, both require spending energy and Mother Nature hates to spend energy and will avoid doing so wherever and whenever possible. In the case of electron pairing, if they have the same spins (both positive or both negative) they just won't pair up in the same orbital unless an enormously large amount of energy is supplied. And the way that we now know Mother, she won't spend it unless under very extreme and "unearthly" conditions such as those found in the core of a type of super-sized collapsing star called white dwarfs (reference 11 of this chapter has some good info on this) (11).

Atomic Orbitals Revisited – In Chapter 2, I talked about orbitals, the part of space around an atomic nucleus where there is a positive probability for electrons to be found. I also told you about Schrödinger Equation that can calculate the values of these probabilities. In simple language, orbitals are invisible but mathematically well-defined electron "cages" surrounding atomic nuclei. If an electron is to associate with any given atomic nucleus, the only way to do it is to enter one of these cages at any given time. And, as we shall see later, even entering a cage has to follow certain and definite rules, depending on what stage of an atom's construction an electron is joining in. Four different types of atomic orbitals have been discovered so far and have been assigned the symbols "s", "p", "d", and "f", with maximum electron accommodation capacities of 2, 6, 10, and 14, respectively. When completely filled, the electrons are arranged in pairs of opposite spins, and as such, each s, p, d, and f orbital could accommodate, respectively, 1, 3, 5, and 7 pairs of electrons with opposite spins. The energy level of each orbital is shown by the *Principal Quantum Number*, n, preceding the orbital's symbol. The value of "n" increases as you get farther from the nucleus so that the higher this value, the higher the energy of the corresponding orbital. The number of electrons contained in each orbital is shown by a superscripted number at the upper right corner of the symbol. Thus, $2s^1$ describes an "s" orbital at the second energy level ($n = 2$) with respect to the corresponding atomic nucleus, which contains 1 electron.

Hund's Rule — We hopefully remember that atoms are a combination of nuclei and electrons, and now also know that electrons are confined into a special part of space around the nuclei called orbitals. According to Hund's Rule, for any p, d, and f set of atomic orbitals with the same energy level (that is equal values for "n"), all unoccupied ones will have to be partially filled with the first available electron before the second electron could enter with an opposite spin *(12)*.

The (n+l) Rule — The order in which these orbitals are filled is governed by the *(n + l) Rule*, also known either as the *Madelung Rule* (after the German physicist, Erwin Madelung, 1881-1972) or the *Klechkovsky Rule* (after the Russian chemist, Vsevolod Klechkovsky, 1900-1972). The term "*l*" in this formula is called the *"Azimuthal Quantum Number"*, which takes up different values for each specific type of orbital. These values for s, p, d, and f orbitals are 0, 1, 2, and 3, respectively.

Now let's go back to the Aufbau principle: According to the Aufbau principle the order of the electrons filling atomic orbitals progresses according to the increase in the energies of the orbitals. In other words, orbitals with lower energy are occupied first. Figure 1 shows a schematic representation of this principle. If we substitute the corresponding numerical values (as described above) for "n" and "l", we should see that all the orbitals falling on the same arrow in Figure 1 have the same (n + l) value. For example, the 3rd arrow from the top covers 2p and 3s orbitals. Substituting l = 1 for the p and l = 0 for the s orbital, the n + l for both will turn out to be 3. Doing the same operation for the first two arrows, 1s and 2s, would result in n + l = 1 and 2, respectively. So, the energy levels of these orbitals increase from 1s to 2s, to 3s. Therefore, any incoming electrons would fill these orbitals in the 1s → 2s → 2p, 3s, according to the Aufbau principle. By the same procedure, t you could see that the orbitals' energy values increase from top (1s, (0 + 1) = 1) to bottom (5f and 6d, (5 + 3) = (6 + 2) = 8), meaning the "filling" of the atomic system of Figure 1 begins with the (1s) set and ends with the (5f, 6d) set of orbitals. Moreover, the direction of the arrows in Figure 1 point to the direction of the order of the orbital filling processes.

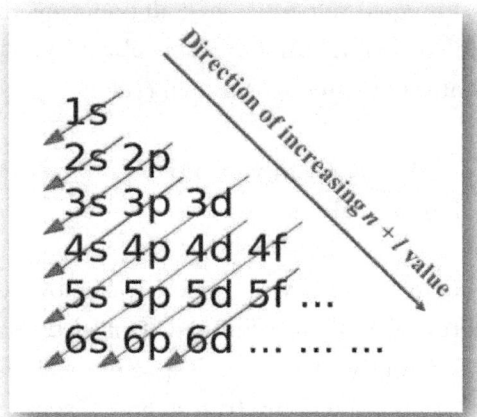

Figure 1. The Aufbau Principle: Order in which orbitals are arranged by increasing energy according to the Madelung rule and exemplifying one of the "by-rule" working mechanisms of Nature. Each diagonal arrow corresponds to a different value of $n + l$. Figure credit.[2]

The Aufbau principle demonstrates an organized mechanism for a stepwise formation of atoms by progressively adding electrons to go from a smaller atom to a larger one. Each addition places each electron in its *most stable* state with respect to *both* the central nucleus *and* the present electrons. The Aufbau method seems to be able to satisfy experimental observations and holds for neutral atoms as well as for ions and molecules.

As is the case with some other natural phenomena, there are some exceptions to the execution of this principle. There is one section in the Periodic Table known as Transition Metals whose members are, well, metals, and of which there are 58. Nineteen of these (about 16% of the total number of elements in the Periodic Table) do not obey the Madelung Rule (*12*). These exceptions were noticed because their experimentally detected electronic configurations did not match those predicted by the Medlung Rule. However, scientists have shown that the electronic configuration for these exceptional elements could be figured out by the use of a mathematical methodology called Hyper Hartree-Fock equations (*12*). In either case, Nature follows strict and solidly determined rules for self-government.

A mini-take-home conclusion from the Aufbau principle — The reason I call this section a "mini-take-home" is that we will have an extended conclusion section later on in this book. For right now, though, let me draw your attention to the very important conclusion that the Aufbau Principle relays to us: The build-up of our Universe is not a random process. Rather, it is a stepwise and pattern-following procedure that is dictated by the logic inherent in the heart of the existence of each single particle of matter and in each quanta of energy (more in Chapters 13 and 14). In atomic constructions, each electron finds its own "home" in a space around the atomic nucleus which has been separated from the rest by *no* visible partitions, as if they *know* where they have to go. And they keep adding in that order until a highly specialized atomic element has been made with its own unique characteristics. And when the Element is made, the electrons stop coming. No more additions. The *Door* is closed. Sounds supernatural, doesn't it? Sounds ready for somebody to jump right in and uses this phenomenon, like many others, to set shop to sell *"Guidance"*, doesn't it? And worst of all, it does sound familiar...doesn't it?

But, good news: There is nothing supernatural! This amazing, yet highly ordered, process is guided by the information that electrons inherit within themselves and information received from the nuclei of their "home atoms". Depending on the number of protons and neutrons and the number of electrons, the nature of the product elements is "determined" (again, more in Chapters 13 and 14). If there is one proton in the nucleus, there will be one orbital (1s) which can accommodate only one electron, and the element is called hydrogen. If there are 6 protons and 6 neutrons in the nucleus, the resulting "nuclear" information will call for, and admits, only 6 electrons into the system, two each, in three orbitals (1s, 2s, and 2p), and the element carbon is born. The Aufbau Principle will be obeyed.

We will have a more detailed discussion on this phenomenon of *"Ordered Synthesis"* of our world but here I just wanted to relay to you the "mini-take-home conclusion", the fact that the very basic building blocks of Life have been, and are being, created through absolutely precise and determined processes, and that the language that these processes are written in is the "exact art" of mathematics.

Notes

[1] Thales of Miletus (*circa* 624-546 BCE) was a philosopher, astronomer, and mathematician, known as one of the Greek Seven Sages from Miletus in Asia Minor, part of the ancient Persian Empire.

[2] Credit for Figure 1: Scheme of Madelung Rule.jpg, User: Goodphy / Wikimedia Commons / CC-BY-SA 4.0
Attribution: By Goodphy (Own work) [CC BY-SA 4.0 [http://creativecommons.org/licenses/by-sa/4.0)], via Wikimedia Commons
Page URL: https://commons.wikimedia.org/wiki/File%3AScheme_of_Madelung_Rule.jpg
File URL: https://upload.wikimedia.org/wikipedia/commons/e/ec/Scheme_of_Madelung_Rule.jpg

References

1. NASA, *Planck Mission Brings Universe into Sharp Focus*, March 2013. URL: https://www.nasa.gov/mission_pages/planck/news/planck20130321.html
2. Schrödinger E, An Undulatory Theory of the Mechanics of Atoms and Molecules, *Phys Rev*, 28 (6), 1049-1070, 1926.
3. Mendelejew D, *Über die Beziehungen der Eigenschaften zu den Atomgewichten der Elemente, Zeit Chem*, 405–406, 1869.
4. International Union of Pure and Applied Chemistry (IUPAC): IUPAC Announces the Names of the Elements 113, 115, 117, and 118 IUPAC, 2016, URL: https://iupac.org/iupac-announces-the-names-of-the-elements-113-115-117-and-118/
5. St. Fleur N, Four New Names Officially Added to the Periodic Table of Elements, *The* New York Times, December, 2016. URL: https://www.nytimes.com/2016/12/01/science/periodic-table-new-elements.html?_r=0
6. SchneiderP, Ehlers J, Falco EE, *Gravitational Lenses, Springer-Verlag, New York, 1992.*
7. Schröder KP, Smith RC, Distant future of the Sun and Earth revisited, *Mont Not Roy Astro Soc*, 386 (1): 155, 2008.
8. Veltman M, Facts and Mysteries in Elementary Particle Physics, *World Sci*, ISBN 981-238-149-X, 2003.
9. *Close F, Neutrinos,* Oxford University Press, 2010, ISBN: 0-199-69599-7.
10. Massimi M, *Pauli's Exclusion Principle,* Cambridge University Press, ISBN 0-521-83911-4, 2005.
11. Koberlein B, A Supernova's Tale, *One Universe at a Time*, 2 April 2014. URL: *https://briankoberlein.com/2014/04/02/supernovas-tale/*
12. Engel T and Reid P, *Physical Chemistry*, Pearson Benjamin-Cummings, pp. 477–479, 2006, ISBN 080533842X.

CHAPTER 4

Chemical Bonds and Molecules

—⚹—

THERE IS HARDLY ANY OF us who has not heard the word *"molecule"*. Nevertheless, there may be a percentage of the "heard" crowd who may still ask "what *is* a molecule anyway?" By definition, a molecule is a form of matter which is produced by bonding together of two or more atoms. From a chemistry and physics point of view, the word "bonding" could have more than one meaning, or more accurately, more than one mechanism. When you use the magnet tomato to post your water bill on your refrigerator, it's because the magnet and the metal door of the fridge bond by virtue of their electromagnetic characters. Or when you glue back together the broken pieces of your favorite china, you utilize the bonding between the pieces of the china and the glue. As a third example, you could consider the bonding between sugar granules and water molecules when you watch the crystals disappear into the hot liquid as you stir the mixture in your coffee cup. You do still have the sweet stuff in your cup but you can't see it anymore. It's because the sugar molecules have tightly associated themselves with those of water, although chemically speaking, both the sugar and the water are still exactly the very same compounds that they were before this mixing. The only reason we do not see the sugar after getting dissolved is that the sugar molecules love those of water so much that they leave each other to "hug" the water's. And the separation makes them invisible because now they are a bunch of microscopic particles (called molecules) too small to be detected by our naked eyes. While these types of association could be considered some *types* of "bonding", they are not of the kind that makes molecules from atoms. Some people like to classify these as *physical bonds* resulting from electromagnetic attraction between, for example, the surfaces of a magnet and a metal (iron) or electrostatic attraction between the glue and the pieces of your broken china, or sugar crystals and water. In essence, physical bonds form because of opposing characters of the bonding parts. Magnetic attractions would be between the opposing moments (north pole-south pole) of two magnetic pieces. Electrostatic bonding (such as sugar and water) result from attractions of opposing electrical charges, in this case negatively charged oxygen and positively charged hydrogen atoms in both compounds. One of the characteristics of physical bonding is reversibility. You could easily pull the tomato magnet away from the fridge, and with a little effort, you could also separate the glued pieces of china after having a spirited conversation with your Significant Other. In the case of your cup of coffee, you can recover the sugar component by carefully boiling off the water and get your sweets back, as long as it's not overheated to the caramelization point, because at that point you will have some other compounds as well due to some chemical changes. This reversibility of physical bonds could sometimes work to our advantage too. Just imagine the Band-Aid® you stuck on the little shave cut on your husband's face, which by the way works by an electrostatic attraction between his skin and the glue on the Band-Aid®, would never come off. Would that bonding have been irreversible, he might have looked like a bulletin board after a few weeks.

The interested reader is referred to the large number of literature sources for information on the nature of molecular binding or physical bonds and mechanisms of their formation.

The kinds of bonds that hold together the constituent atoms in molecules are called *Chemical Bonds*. Chemical bonds are electromagnetic or electronic in nature and I will get to them later on in this chapter but before starting the bonding discussion itself, let's learn some more definitions of the terms which may come handy in our understanding of these bonds:

Valence electrons (VEs) - VEs are electrons that atoms use to make bonds with each other. With the exception of transition metals, valence electrons are located in the outermost atomic shells with respect to the nucleus.

Electronegativity - Electronegativity is a measure of how strongly an atom attracts electrons to itself *(1)*. I should remind you again that electrons are negatively charged particles. The term was introduced in 1932 by the great chemist and two-times Nobel laureate, Linus Pauling (1901-1994) as part of his propositions of chemical bonds theories. This affinity is not equal for all the elements of the Periodic Table and is a balance between the number of protons in the nucleus (the atomic number) which are positively charged, and the electronic configuration around the nucleus for any given atom. Putting it in a simpler way, electronegativity is directly proportional to how well the negatively charged valence electrons are shielded from the positively charged nucleus by other electrons. In the Periodic Table, the most and the least electronegative elements are fluorine (F) and francium (Fr), respectively.

Electropositivity - As apparent from its name, this is the opposite of electronegativity. It is a measure of the tendency of an atom or a molecule to give up electrons to other atoms or molecules.

Now let's return to our discussion on chemical bonds, starting with those having an electromagnetic nature. Electromagnetic attractions (or forces) are operational when two or more opposite electric charges are placed in close proximity. One of the best examples of electromagnetic attractions is that between atomic nuclei and their surrounding electrons. This attraction keeps electrons in place around the nuclei, thus bringing about the formation of atoms, and therefore, the whole visible universe including the biological life. At microscopic levels, this type of bonding occurs when two atoms with a significant difference in electronegativity react with each other to form a new molecule. Let's take the humble table salt as an example. The tasty crystals are ordered aggregations of molecules made of only two different atoms, sodium (Na) and chlorine (Cl).[1] In its pure form, sodium, an alkaline metal, is really a nasty atom.

Despite its mild appearance and low-key hardness (you can cut it with a butter knife), it's an extremely reactive element. So much so that when you dump a chunk of it in such an otherwise stable liquid as water, it breaks one of the two bonds between hydrogen and oxygen in water (remember the chemical composition of water is H-O-H or the famous H_2O), generating molecular hydrogen (H_2), which spontaneously catches fire. The other product is caustic soda (the well-known drain opener). And when it comes to character, the other molecular component of table salt, chlorine, is not exactly an angel either. The element is a pale-yellow and highly toxic gas that was used in the World War I as one of the early chemical weapons. When breathed, chlorine would form hydrogen chloride (HCl), a very corrosive acid, by reacting with water in the surface mucosa of the lungs. It is not too difficult to imagine the fate of the poor breather.

The other characteristics of these two elements, which play key roles in their forming table salt, are the very low and very high electronegativity of Na and Cl, respectively. In fact, you may say that, compared to Cl, Na is an electropositive atom.

In the process of salt formation, sodium gives up its only valence electron to chlorine. Since electron has a negative charge, the originally neutral chlorine becomes negatively charged by gaining sodium's electron while sodium becomes positively charged due to the loss of that negative electron (it now has one *less* negative charge). So, when these natively neutral elements become inversely charged ions[2], the consequence based on the laws of electromagnetism is obvious: They attract each other. And not only that, they hold on to each other very tightly, as if they are in a very electromagnetic love! Or, picturing the attraction in a less romantic way, the electronically "poor" sodium now has to follow the electronically "rich" chlorine to wherever it goes. It is this tight "hugging" of these two ions that produces table salt with all of its amazing taste-enhancing properties. In physical sciences, this type of bonding is called *"ionic bonding"*. Ionic bonds play important roles in nature. All types of salts, just like table salt, are ionic. These include all the electrolytes in our blood which are vital to our health, survival, and the normal functioning of our bodies. Another important example of the role of ionic bonds in Nature is that of the salts dissolved in oceans and other natural salt water resources, which modulate the right functioning of the food chain that maintains the survival of animals all the way up to that of our own.

Now let's look at the other type of chemical bonding, those without apparent electric charges although they are still formed by electronic interactions. These are called *"covalent bonds"*. As was described earlier, atoms are made of nuclei and electrons with the latter confined in orbitals (those virtual electron cages). While not all chemical elements of the Periodic Table are capable of forming covalent bonds, in those which are, it is done by coming together of valence electrons (VEs). Like most humans who believe the life would be more enjoyable (at least sometimes) if they could pair up with a "better half", valence electrons too like to pair up with theirs.[3]

And it is this "better half-better half" coupling that generates covalent bonds. In the electrons' world, better halves are those electrons with opposite spins, or an electronic version of animals' opposite sexes. And if they can't do it within their own atomic system, they seek their mate in other atoms. This nature of VEs is the very basis of molecule formation, and in turn, constitutes one of the elementary steps in the formation of biological life. Perhaps one of the most well-known examples of molecule formation is the taken-for-granted compound we hardly ever bother to appreciate until we ran short of it: The water molecule. Most of us know that water, which I would like to thankfully remember as "The Solvent of Life", is composed of two atoms of hydrogen and one atom of oxygen. In this case, each of the two unpaired VEs of oxygen pair up with the single VE of each hydrogen atom to form the V-shaped water molecule in which the oxygen is the tip of the "V" and the two arms are covalent bonds that hold on to one hydrogen each. The amazing consequence of this coupling is a significant change in the physicochemical properties of the two elements: The process of electron pairing, and the formation of two new covalent bonds in this case turns two gases, one highly flammable (hydrogen) and the other an extremely reactive and corrosive one (oxygen), into a clear, odorless, tasteless, and soothing liquid, so chemically inert that the delicate biological processes of life could begin, flourish, and be sustained in it.

Although ionic bonds are absolutely important in the formation and sustention of our world, the importance of covalent bonding could not be overemphasized either. The kinds of matter that makes up most parts of the structure of biologically living organisms is made by the formation of covalent bonds: Proteins (such as musculoskeletal structures in animals) and cellulose (the plants' main structural element) are made mostly by formation of covalent bonds between different types of atoms and molecules. So are most of the man-made materials which we use every single day: Plastics, medicines, paints, artificial fabrics, are mostly covalently bonded compounds. This type of bonding is neutral, that is, it carries no electrical charges although some forms of it may be only partially polarized. Covalent bonds are usually stable bonds. This stability is of utmost importance when it comes to the development and sustention of the biological life. Just imagine the disaster that may occur if the wood framing of a house suddenly loses the stability of the cellulose covalent bonds that are holding the whole structure together. Or if one day we wake up and find out that all the covalent bonds of all the proteins that made up the body of our beloved pet doggy have decided to not be stable anymore. On that fateful morning, we would find nothing but a pile of free amino acids powder, the building blocks of the doggy's muscles, skin, and fur proteins, on the living room couch. These are, of course, only hypothetical scenarios but they could at least demonstrate the importance of covalent bonding in Nature and in our lives.

It is very important to notice that, just as in atomic electrons that have to reside only within atomic orbitals, electrons that form covalent bonds could only exist in *molecular orbitals (MOs)*. MOs are similar to atomic orbitals described before (Chapter 3 and this chapter) except they are formed by the association of the VEs of at least two interacting atoms. As two or more atomic nuclei (either as free atoms or as parts of molecules) approach each other, so do their valence electrons that are still in their orbital cages. Under the right conditions, the atomic orbitals overlap and form new orbitals, the MOs, and thus, new molecules. There are two major theories for the general description, analyses, and calculations of molecular orbitals. One is called the *Valence Bond Theory (VBT)*, proposed for the first time in 1927 by Walter Heitler (1904-1981) and Fritz London (1900-1954), and further developed by Linus Pauling shortly after (1928 and 1930) (2). The other one is *Molecular Orbital Theory (MOT)* originally developed by Friedrich Hund (1896-1997),

Robert Mulliken (1896-1986), John C. Slater (1900-1976), and John Lennard-Jones (1894-1954) *(2)*. Quantum mechanical methodologies, and Erwin Schrödinger's wave functions in particular, were utilized in the development of both VBT and MOT. Going into an in-depth description of these theories is out of the scope of this book but let me suffice by saying that VBT proposes a rather *localized* and more rigid electronic bonding model, one electron pair at a time, while MOT suggests that molecular bonds are *delocalized* and their effect is spread almost all over the molecule. In either case, the electronic orbitals from each parent atom have to *overlap* in order for a new bond to form.

So, what is the use of all this information? Does this knowledge of molecular creation through molecular bond formation, proposed by such brilliant minds using such complicated science, serve any purpose of our concern? The answer is "absolutely". No matter which of the two theories we use, the juice of the whole set of findings tells us that, just like in the case of formation of atoms, the coming to existence of molecules, and I mean *any* molecule, from water to our bodies, would be possible if and only if the parent atoms could meet strict electronic requirements such as spin and energy. I would like to refer these requirements as *"quantum match factors (QMFs)"*. As we will see in later chapters, it is the strict guidance of these rules, and the strict obedience of these rules by the participating components, that create the deterministic nature of our World. So any information regarding these rules and mechanisms would be helpful to guide us towards the final conclusion of these writings.

Of course, for any molecule-forming reaction to start and go to completion, there are also a set of ambient requirements which have to be met, such as the right temperature, pressure, medium, or concentration of the reactants and products, or in a general term, the *"environmental conditions"*. But without the existence of the just-right QMFs, the existence of these conditions, whatever they may be, would be of no constructive effects. The nature and effects of the environmental factors are discussed in Chapter 6.

Another important factor for molecular bond formation is symmetry. Two VE-containing orbitals have to have compatible symmetries to be able to overlap and make a molecule. This is another strict and uncompromising prerequisite for bond formation. So, what is this new term "symmetry"? There are quite a few meanings and definitions for the word, depending what context you want to define it in. There are manifestations of symmetry in almost any aspect of life, not only in chemistry and bond formation, but also in mathematics, biology, physics, art, sociology, and even religion (3, 4). It is quite an important word in the Nature's dictionary and one of the means through which all the components of the world at large may communicate with each other.

In lay language, symmetry means topological homogeneity, harmony and proportionality. It is also a kind of balance among the parts of a composite system. Consider a perfectly spherical object with a perfectly smooth and unmarked surface. If you look at it, then close your eyes and somebody turns it without telling you, be it a slight few-degrees turn or a complete 180° turn, to the left or to the right, upward or downward, you can never tell if anything had been done to the sphere when you open your eyes back up. It still looks exactly the same, even after the turns, because an unmarked sphere is fully symmetrical all around. Not all shapes and objects are fully symmetrical however. If the car you just parked in the driveway is turned around while you were inside watching TV, you could immediately tell your teenager had been up to something when you come back outside. Because a car does not have a full symmetry, you could easily tell if there is any change in its original position. The human body has a good bit of symmetry with respect to an imaginary plane, perpendicular to the width of the body, passing centrally and longitudinally through the head and the trunk, and in between the legs. With respect to this plane, called a *"plane of symmetry"*, and from outside only, the right side and the left are, at least macroscopically, very closely similar (I do not use the word *"identical"* in this particular example as it would be an exaggeration, although in symmetry *"identicality"* is a requirement). Now if you pass the plane of symmetry through the body in such a way that it separates the front (anterior) side from the back (posterior) side of the body, you can readily see that there is no symmetry. The anterior of our bodies thankfully look very different from its posterior.

Symmetry is an immensely important concept in Nature and has critical importance in the formation of biological life and evolution of species. According to the modern astrophysics, two symmetry-related events started the process of creation of our Universe. The first one was the breach of symmetry in the initial tiny energy bubble which led to the occurrence of the Big Bang (Chapter 2). As of today, the reason for this event is not known and probably will not be known until the firm establishment of the Holy Grail of quantum physics (or of Science at large for that matter), *The Grand Unified Theory of Quantum Gravity* (5).

The second symmetry breach was the matter-antimatter imbalance which resulted in the formation of the material universe as we know it today and are part of. Some of us may be familiar with Einstein's famous, and equally ingenious equation, $E = mc^2$. Although relatively simple in appearance, this equation mathematically describes a very important and fundamental rule of Nature: Energy and matter are, in fact, the same phenomena and are also interconvertible. Under the right conditions, matter can turn into energy, and energy can turn into matter. As described in Chapter 2, the latter event, the energy-to-matter conversion, happened shortly after the start of the Big Bang (and I mean really shortly, within 10^{-32} seconds or 0.32 seconds with 30 zeros after the decimal point), and here you are reading this book. So, what does formation of the material world have to do with symmetry? The answer: Everything! Let me explain: Quantum physical calculations, as well as experimental data, show that in its conversion, energy not only produces matter but it also generates *antimatter* in equal quantities. Conversely, in an equally beautiful process, when matter and antimatter meet, they produce energy in a combine-and-destroy process called *"annihilation"*. So, if energy produces *equal* numbers of matter/antimatter pairs, and the pairs are completely destroyed due to annihilation, how in the world the first matter, and therefore our Universe and ourselves, were formed during the Big Bang when every particle of produced matter was annihilated by a particle of antimatter? Again, nothing supernatural. Here is where the symmetry, or better said its breach (asymmetry), comes into play. Calculations on the present-day CMB (cosmic microwave background) radiation (covered in Chapter 2) and the matter content of the universe, have concluded that shortly after the Big Bang there was an asymmetry in the matter/antimatter balance in the order of 1/1,000,000,000 (1 out of 1 billion). This means for every 1 billion matter/antimatter pairs generated from every billion photons (packets of energy in the form of light, described in Chapter 13), there was 1 particle of matter too many. To simplify further, this means for each 1 billion (1,000,000,000) *antimatter* particles produced by each billion photons, there were 1 billion-and-one (1,000,000,001) particles of matter. As there were not a matching rival antimatter particle to destroy that one extra matter particle, matter could not be annihilated 100% and amounted to what is now the material Universe we see, touch, and in general, feel around us. And yes, we ourselves are part of it. This asymmetry in matter-antimatter balance was itself the result of yet another symmetry breach in the decay pattern of an elementary particle called the *Kaon* or *neutral meson*, K^0 (6). The good news is that, that subject is way beyond the scope of this book and shall not be discussed in here any further.

Another condition for the formation of molecules is that the level of energies of the overlapping atomic orbitals have to be close. Every orbital in an atom or a molecule has its own level of energy and those orbitals containing valence electrons are no exceptions. So, when two valence orbitals are approaching to make a bond, the difference in their energy levels will determine the feasibility of formation of the new bond. The smaller that difference, the higher the probability of bonding and formation of a new molecule.

So, even with all these symmetry and energy requirements satisfied, what makes two (or more) atoms to combine and form new molecules anyway? In other words, what is the driving force behind the molecular formation process? Why are the *"reactive"* atoms not happy as they are and seek to become molecules? The answer is in another rule of Nature: On a relative basis, a low-energy state is more stable, and therefore more favorable, than a high-energy state. And this holds true in both microscopic *and* macroscopic worlds. Let's look at a macroscopic-world example: What would happen if you picked up a pebble from your backyard, took it with you to the rooftop of your home, held out your arm above the backyard and let go of the pebble? It drops right back down to the ground. Right? Of course. A perfect no-brainer. But why? Because of the Earth's gravity you say? Sure. Another no-brainer. But, again, why? What does the gravity do to the pebble that makes it drops down, apparently without having any choices? The answer is that the inherent *potential energy* content of the pebble increased as you took it from the backyard (the *ground state*) to the rooftop (the *excited state*). Nothing visibly changed in the little rock, but believe it or not, its potential energy grew higher on the rooftop as it worked its way up *against* the Earth's gravity. "Something" is aware of anything that happens to anything. Here, you may consider Mother Nature as a very rich lady. Rich in energy, that is. But this lady is at the same time highly observant of what she loans you. She will take it back soon as the time and the condition is right. So, when you let go of the pebble in your hand, it will give back the energy it gained by falling right back to the ground where you picked it up from. Who paid for this process? You did. You spent energy to pick the pebble off the ground, carry it to the rooftop, and drop it. To do all that, you had to spend some of the energy that you had stored in your body when you ate your last meal. You may say "ok, next time I'll use my elevator to climb to the rooftop so I don't have to spend my own energy and get the act done for free." You could but you still have to pay for the electricity that moves your elevator. And to pay for the electricity, you'll have to work to earn that money. And to do the work, you'll have to spend energy. And to gain that energy you have to, guess what? ...eat! There is no scape. There *is* no free lunch in the Lady's world.

As mentioned above, energy payback events occur in the microscopic systems too. Most of us have seen those glow-in-the-dark toys and objects. We probably have also noticed that, for the glowing process, they need no batteries neither do they generate any heat when they glow, like do regular light bulbs. This phenomenon is generally referred to as *"luminescence"* a term coined by the German physicist E.E.G. Wiedemann (1852-1928) in 1888. What happens is some of the electrons of the material absorb energy from a source, in this case the photons of the visible light from a light source. In a process comparable to that of the backyard pebble, the energetically excited electrons jump from their ground state orbitals (the backyard) to an excited state orbital (the rooftop). Since, energetically, this is not a stable position for the electrons, they will drop back to their ground state orbital soon as the source of energy (the light) is disrupted or lowered in intensity. But since the Lady never forgets what she had given to those electrons, they have to give her back the loan, in this case the energy they absorbed to get "high" (high in orbital level that is). That paid-back energy is the green-, red-, purple-, *etc.*-colored glow we see in the dark. By giving off the extra energy, the electrons go back to their lower energy, and therefore more stable, ground state and stay there happily until the next jolt is delivered.

The very same rule, that the lower the energy of a system, the more stable that system would be, is the driving force for formation of molecules as well. Again, recall that when atoms bind together their valence orbitals couple and mix to form *molecular* orbitals. According to the MOT (described above) when atoms and molecules react to make new molecules, they do so because the molecular orbitals of the products are lower in energy (and therefore more stable) than each atomic or molecular orbital of the reactants.

So, we could safely conclude that, just as in the case of formation of atoms, formation of molecules follows strict natural laws too. Certain and well-defined requirements have to be fulfilled before a molecule could come into existence.

Overall, the final outcome of any chemical reaction, that is, the nature and properties of the final products, would be defined by two main criteria: 1. The chemical structure(s) of the product(s), determined by the order of connections among the participating atoms, and 2. The overall 3-dimensional *"shape"* of the product molecule(s). In chemistry these structures are referred to as the *"primary"* and the *"secondary"* structures of molecules, respectively. We shall review these and other structural variations in the next chapter.

Notes

[1] The reason for sodium is abbreviated as Na (and not, say, So or Sd) is that the Swedish chemist, Jons Jakob Berzelius (1779-1848), in his development of atomic abbreviations, used the Latin name *Natrium* (itself taken from the Egyptian Natron) for sodium.

[2] Ions are atoms or molecules that have lost or gained electrons. When electrons are lost, the positive atom or molecule is called a *cation*. When electrons are gained, the negative atom or molecule is called an *anion*.

[3] It may be interesting to note that these rules, pairing up of the electrons in covalent bonds and those of the electron-poor sodium and electron-rich chlorine of table salt, are followed all the way up to the processes that control our lives too.

REFERENCES

1. Jensen WB, Electronegativity from Avogadro to Pauling: Part 1: Origins of the Electronegativity Concept, *J Chem Ed*, 73 (1): 11–20, 1996.
2. Murrel JN, Kettle SFA, Tedder JM, *The Chemical* Bond, John *Wiley & Sons*, 2nd Ed, 1985, ISBN 0-471-90759-6.
3. Weyl H, *Symmetry*, Princeton University Press, SBN 0-691-02374-3, 1982.
4. Hill CT and Lederman LM, *Symmetry and the Beautiful Universe*, Prometheus Books, 2005.
5. Hawking SW, *The Theory of Everything: The Origin and Fate of the Universe*, Phoenix Books, 2006, ISBN 978-1-59777-508-3.
6. Beringer J, *et al.*, Particle Data Group, PR D86, 010001, 2012. URL: http://pdg.lbl.gov

CHAPTER 5

Higher-Order Structures and Molecular Shapes

—⚛—

ONE METHOD OF CLASSIFICATIONS OF molecular structure in science is based on the nature of the bonds involved. Within this context, I define "bond" as the *interactions* among atoms in a molecule that determine the final and overall shape and properties of that molecule. This definition is a broad-spectrum one to include all types of chemical bonds, from ionic to covalent, and polar or neutral. In addition to determining the 3-dimensional shape of molecules, bonds could determine their functionality too. This is particularly important in molecules with biological activity as we shall see later in this chapter. So, let's take a look at the different molecular structures which may result from these interactions:

Primary Structures (structures of the first kind). The structure resulted from the bonding of constituent atoms in the main backbone of a molecule is referred to as the primary structure. The constituent atoms may all be of one kind or of different kinds. Molecules made of two A atoms (AA) or two B atoms (BB) or one of each (AB, or BA) all have a *diatomic* (made of two atoms) primary structures. Molecules made of, for example, six of these (A *or* B and in *any* order and ratio) will have *hexa-atomic* (made of six atoms) primary structures and so on. The scope of the primary structure ends here, it is simply the fashion in which the *"core"* atoms in a molecule are connected with one another. Any other structural feature falls into the category of higher-order structural definitions described below *(1)*. It should be noted, however, that the higher-order structures of any molecule are still entirely related, and a function of, the primary structure of that molecule as I shall explain below.

Before I discussed the higher-order structures, it might be helpful to go over some preliminary information for a better understanding of the subject:

1. *Organic Molecules.* Organic molecules are molecules that are involved in either the structure or the sustenance, or both, of the life of biologically living organisms and contain carbon as their core element. In contrast, *inorganic* molecules are those which are not directly involved in the structure of living organisms although some *may* contain carbon. The majority of inorganic molecules are composed of elements other than carbon. The science dealing with the making and properties of organic compounds is called *organic chemistry*.
2. *Carboxylic Acids.* Carboxylic acids are organic acids (as opposed to inorganic acids like sulfuric acid, the car battery acid) which are mainly compounds which contain one or more carboxylic acid functional group. Carboxylic functional groups are represented as COOH, or CO_2H, found in a large number of natural and synthetic compounds, and are the acid functionality of amino acids, the building blocks of proteins.
3. *Amines.* Amines are organic molecules containing one or more amine groups. Amine groups are nitrogen-containing functionalities that come in three classes of primary, secondary,

and tertiary structures. The primary amine group is shown as NH_2 and is the amine functionality of amino acids.

4. *Amino Acids.* Amino acids, as the name implies, are organic molecules that contain one or more of both acid and amine groups. Although there are 500 or so known amino acids, only a certain member of these are the building blocks of genetically coded natural proteins (discussed in Chapter 7). The general structure of proteinogenic (protein-making) amino acids is shown below:

$$H_2N\text{-}CH(R)\text{-}CO_2H$$

where R, is called the "amino acid side chain" in chemistry and can be different chemical groups which is specific to each individual amino acid. For example, in the simplest of proteinogenic amino acids, glycine, R is a hydrogen. There are only 22 different R groups, and thus 22 different proteinogenic amino acids found in prokaryotes (single-celled organisms with no cellular nuclei) and eukaryotic cells (cells that have nuclei such as human cells) (*2, 3*). Of these, 20 are coded by the species-specific genomes of all organisms and 2 by prokaryotic organisms (*4*) (Chapter 7).

5. *Hydrogen Bonds.* A hydrogen bond is an electrostatic attraction between hydrogen atoms and more electronegative atoms such as oxygen, nitrogen, and sulfulr. The bond may form both *intramolecularly* (within the same molecule) and *intermolecularly* (among different molecules). Hydrogen bonds are simply an electrostatic "through-space" type of attraction, and as such, are virtual in contrast to covalent bonds which form by direct participation of electrons and with well-established molecular orbitals. Hydrogen bonds may be considered a weak version of ionic bonds.

6. *Hydrophilic Molecules.* From *hydr* (Greek: water) and *philia* (Greek: love), in chemistry hydrophilic molecules refer to molecules that attract, attach to, or dissolve in water, such as honey and table salt. Compounds that are hydrophilic are usually *polar*, that is, they carry an overall full or partial positive and/or negative electric charge.
7. *Hydrophobic Molecules.* From *hydr* and *phobia* (Greek: fear) in chemistry hydrophobic molecules refer to molecules that repel, and are immiscible with, water, such as bee wax and cooking oil. Compounds that are hydrophobic are usually *non-polar*, that is, they carry no overall electric charges.

Keeping the above definitions in mind, now let's go back to our discussion on higher-order molecular structures:

Secondary Structures (structures of the second kind). Although the higher-order structures (HOSs) are mostly defined for, and studied in the context of, proteins and nucleic acids (the gene-related molecules, discussed in Chapter 7), they can be encountered in other areas of natural sciences. Since proteins provide the most straightforward and frequently encountered examples, I shall use proteins in our introduction to the HOSs. As mentioned above, natural proteins are formed from 22 different types of amino acids (2, 3, 4). The primary chain-like structure of proteins is made from head-to-tail attachments between amino acids where the acid (CO_2H) function of one amino acid is covalently bonded to the amine (NH_2) function of another as shown below:

….HN-CH(R^1)-CO-NH-CH(R^2)-CO-…..-NH-CH(R^n)-CO ….

where R^1, R^2, …., R^n, are any of the 22 proteinogenic amino acid side chains. The shown structure represents only *a section* of a protein molecule. The rest of the molecular chain is omitted for simplicity and represented only by the dots. Moreover, the CO-NH bonds that connect the amino acids are called *"peptide bonds"*. Those of us with good eyes might have noticed that in the shown structure, the acid (CO_2H) and the amine (NH_2) groups have been changed to "CO" and "NH" groups, respectively, after the formation of the peptide bond. This is because any coupling of two amino acids through a peptide bond is accompanied by elimination of a water molecule (H_2O). So, if you do the additions and subtractions, you'll see that you'll end up only with a CONH group.

Now, although the primary structure of proteins is a straight chain of amino acids bound together like the links of a chain, in reality they never stay (or exist) as straight and rod-like molecules. Rather, intra- and intermolecular interactions among different chemical groups, from either the peptide bonds or from the amino acids' sidechains, cause the molecule as a whole to assume different overall 3-dimensional shapes. These *interactions* are of electrostatic nature and may be attractive or repulsive interactions. To picture the situation, you may consider the attraction and repulsion between the like and opposite poles of two magnet bars. An example of an attractive interaction is formation of hydrogen bonds between the oxygen atoms and hydrogen atoms of peptide bonds (CO-NH). The more electronegative (Chapter 3) oxygens attract the less electronegative hydrogens. In some cases when this happens intramolecularly in a long chain of a protein, the result would be a helical structure called an alpha helix (α-helix). Alternatively, formation of hydrogen bonds among parallel and adjacent chains (*i.e.*, intermolecular attractions) leads to another structure called beta sheet (β-sheet). These types of structures are generally referred to as secondary structures. Note that they are different from, but still a function of, a molecule's primary structure.

Tertiary Structures (structures of the third kind). Hydrophilicity and hydrophobicity were defined above, and I talked about the general structure of amino acids. Upon the completion of the primary and secondary structures, a protein may undergo a third kind of structural rearrangement to form what is called a "tertiary structure". And just as in the case of the secondary, the tertiary structure is also a function of the primary structure, that is, the type of R groups (the amino acid sidechains) *and* the order (or sequence) in which the amino acids are linked together. This may be better illustrated by an inspection of the following structures:

Protein 1: ….HN-CH(R^1)-CO-NH-CH(R^2)-CO-….
Protein 2: ….HN-CH(R^2)-CO-NH-CH(R^1)-CO-….
Protein 3: ….HN-CH(R^3)-CO-NH-CH(R^4)-CO-….
Protein 4: ….HN-CH(R^4)-CO-NH-CH(R^3)-CO-….

Here, sections of 4 different proteins are shown that are made from 4 different amino acids (R^1, R^2, R^3, and R^4). Although each pair (proteins 1 and 2, and proteins 3 and 4) shares the same R groups (that is, same amino acids) each individual protein is different from the other member of the pair due to the different order of linking of the amino acids in the chains (R^1-R^2 *versus* R^2-R^1 and R^3-R^4 *versus* R^4-R^3), or put simply, due to different primary structures. These differences in the primary structures necessarily lead to different proteins, and therefore, to different secondary and tertiary structures. The tertiary structure forms after the formation of the protein's primary and secondary structures. Once the latter two structures are shaped, the molecule "*folds*" itself into a third and final form which is the tertiary structure of the protein. This process is a result of the hydrophobicity of some of the R groups. There are 8 amino acids that carry hydrophobic Rs. Since biological processes occur in an aqueous (watery) environment, which the hydrophobic Rs do not like, a protein that contains a significant number of hydrophobic sidechains would fold in such a way that these groups are pushed into the inner side of the resulting structure so that their contact with the surrounding aqueous environment is minimized. Often, the net result of this process, the so-called tertiary structure, is a globular molecule the surface of which consists of amino acids with hydrophilic Rs (on the surface because they love to mingle with the surrounding water molecules) with those containing hydrophobic Rs forming the inner core of the globule. Examples of this type of structure include hemoglobin and myoglobin, the oxygen-carrying proteins of the vertebrae red blood cells and muscles, respectively (5, 6), and immunoglobulins (also known as antibodies), the proteins produced by the immune system to defend the body against foreign invaders such as bacteria and viruses (7). We shall revisit two of these molecules in the following section.

Quaternary Structures (structures of the fourth kind). In this kind of higher-order structure, two or more macromolecules (or large molecules) such as proteins, nucleic acids (Chapter 7), or carbohydrates (chemical name for sugars), each with its own primary, secondary, and tertiary structures, may aggregate to form still a larger ensemble. The resulting aggregate is called a quaternary structure and the participating proteins are referred to as *"subunits".* Subunits may or may not be the same, that is, they may or may not have the same sequence of amino acids. To qualify for fitting into this category, the molecule must have formed all the primary and secondary bonds and have folded into a tertiary structure. Depending on the nature of the latter structure and functional requirements of the molecule, two or more tertiary structures may come together to form a larger molecule with new physicochemical and biological characteristics. Examples of protein quaternary structures include hemoglobin and myoglobin. In hemoglobin, 2 of each globular protein subunits, called α- and β-subunits, each tightly bound to four non-protein iron-containing molecules called *"heme"*, assemble to form the overall quaternary structure of this oxygen-transferring component of the vertebrae red blood cells. The α and β globular subunits are themselves protein helices (according to their secondary structures) that are stabilized with intramolecular hydrogen bonding (5).

The other example of proteins with quaternary structures is the muscle protein, myoglobin. Unlike hemoglobin, myoglobin has only one iron-containing heme molecule but has a higher affinity for oxygen (6). This higher oxygen affinity is probably due to the fact that myoglobin's function is storing oxygen whereas hemoglobin is an oxygen transporter. The color of red meat is because of the myoglobin-iron bond.

Although divided into two chapters, the material covered in Chapters 4 and 5 are sort of related. Chapter 4 discussed molecules and their formation and chapter 5 showed what else molecules might do with respect to their primary structures. In other words, the material covered in these chapters demonstrated how the function of a molecule is determined by its primary (or core) chemical structure. And as we breeze through the following chapters, you'll see that each chemical structure is itself *determined* by the nature of its predecessors.

References

1. Lee B and Richards FM, The Interpretation of Protein Structures: Estimation of Static Accessibility, *J Mol Biol*, 55 (3): 379-400, 1971.
2. Jakubke H-D and Sewald N, Amino Acids, *Peptides from A to Z: A Concise Encyclopedia*, Wiley-VCH, 2008, ISBN: 9783527621170.
3. Wagner I and Musso H, New Naturally Occurring Amino Acids, *Angew Chem Int Ed Eng*, 22 (11): 816–828, 1983. DOI: 10.1002/anie.198308161
4. Hertweck C, Biosynthesis and Charging of Pyrrolysine, the 22nd Genetically Encoded Amino Acid, *Ang Chem Int Ed Eng*, 50 (41): 9540–9541, 2011.
5. Hardison R, The Evolution of Hemoglobin: Studies of a very ancient protein suggest that changes in gene regulation are an important part of the evolutionary story, *Am Sci*, 87(2): 126, 1999.
6. Ordway GA and Garry DJ, Myoglobin: an essential hemoprotein in striated muscle, *J Exp Biol*, 207 (20): 3441–3446, 2004.
7. Schroeder Jr HW and Cavacini L, Structure and Function of Immunoglobulins, *J Allergy Clin Immunol*, 125 (202): S41-S52, 2010, DOI: 10.1016/j.jaci.2009.09.046

CHAPTER 6

Peripheral Factors in the Formation of Molecules

—∭—

As DISCUSSED ABOVE, MOLECULES ARE primarily made of some combination of atoms, that is, soon as one atom bonds to another, we have a molecule (*1*). If only two atoms do this, we'll have a "diatomic" molecule. If there are three or four atoms, we'll have, respectively, "tri-atomic" and "tetra-atomic" molecules, and so on. Usually, though, when atoms are more than a few, we call them "polyatomic" molecules. For the sake of convenience, and since all chemical elements are, individually speaking, some form of atoms anyway, let's call those making the core of a molecule "internal elements". As discussed above, the shape and properties of any molecule depends primarily on its internal elements. I use the adverb "primarily" because there are also secondary factors that influence how atoms may come together and assemble into molecules. These are the environmental factors which I shall collectively refer to as the "*peripheral factors*". The peripheral factors play key roles, albeit externally, in the initiation, progression, completion, and the overall outcome of chemical reactions. The terms "chemical reaction" or simply "reaction" are used in the chemistry jargon to denote coupling, and assembling, or conversely, decoupling and disassembling of two or more atoms or molecules to form new atoms or molecules.

And the verb for such a process is, of course, *"to react"*. The atoms and molecules that participate in reactions are called *"reactants"* and those that are formed by such reactions are called *"products"*.

Chemical reactions could be factories of Life too. Germination of plant seeds, reproduction of microorganisms, and of plants and higher animals, metabolic processes, and development and even eradication of diseases, are but a few general examples which result from some type of chemical reactions. Any chemical reaction is a function of both the chemical properties of the reactants *and* the peripheral factors that are present at the start and during the progression of that reaction. Of these two, the chemical properties of the reactants (and thus of the internal elements) have the determining role in the initiation and outcome of any reaction. Meaning, if the chemical properties of the reactants are not suitable for a given reaction, that reaction would never commence regardless of the peripheral factors whatever they might be. In biological systems, unfit reactants could result in either distorted chemical reactions or no reaction at all, leading to faulty life-related results or no life at all. And now that we know they are such critical factors, it may be worthwhile to remind ourselves of the fact that the source of chemical properties of any chemical element stems from its electronic structure, that is, the arrangement and configuration of its electrons around the atomic nuclei. They are these electrons that determine whether or not an atom is chemically inert, slightly reactive, or extremely reactive, and also what atoms it is reactive towards. The simplest atom of all elements, hydrogen, reacts violently with the atoms of oxygen to produce water in a reaction we know as "combustion", while helium atoms, the element just next to hydrogen in the Periodic Table (Chapter 4), have no tendency to do so. The reason? A single lonely electron in hydrogen that is so desperate to give itself away to any atom that has the "right stuff" to couple to it, as compared to a *pair* of electrons in helium that are already coupled to each other and happily occupy the same cozy home that we call the 1s (pronounced "one ess") orbital. And such is the story of all physical events in our Universe which bring about progression, change, evolution, and in some cases, Life. The process may be looked at through this mechanism: Some "thing" is not energetically stable (or "happy" in the common language) as it is. Since things have to eventually place themselves in the most stable situation possible, the unhappy thing does so just when the conditions are right. So, as soon as there is a spark of energy to provide the needed initiating energy (which we may call the "ice breaker"), hydrogen and oxygen "hug" each other so tightly that it'll take a lot of energy to break them apart in the molecule their union produced, that is, water. At a universal scale, this process has produced a dynamic, ever-changing world that started from a tiny, timeless, and placeless spot and keeps changing as you read these lines (Chapter 2). But let's not forget that the real face and the real character behind this seemingly chaotic and random look of this world is anything but! Just keep this in mind for the time being until we get to its related discussions in the last two chapters of this book.

Now back to the peripheral factors, what are they and how they affect the fate of chemical reactions: Peripheral factors are the ambient and environmental conditions surrounding the reacting atoms. The main peripheral factors for a typical chemical reaction include temperature, pressure, type of the solvent, and the concentrations of the reactants, and sometimes of the products too (2). So, let's look at these key factors a little more closely:

1. **Pressure.** The pressure factor is important mostly for reactions in the gas phase or the nuclear reactions taking place in the centers of stars such as our own Sun. As such, pressure may not be that important in most solution-phase reactions to which most of chemical reactions, including those of

biological systems, belong. At higher pressures, gaseous atoms or molecules would react faster. This is because at higher pressures, the frequency and the kinetic energy (represented by the temperature, as described below) of molecular collisions (a key factor for a successful chemical reaction) would both be higher. In the case of solid- and solution-phase reactions, pressure usually plays no important role due to the low compressibility of matter in these phases. At the right concentrations, the reactants would be close enough already to react if they could.

2. **Temperature.** The other peripheral factor, temperature, is important as a measure of the kinetic energy which is needed to initiate a reaction and drive it to completion. With some exceptions, every chemical reaction has associated with it a specific amount of energy called the *"activation energy, E_a"*. It is the minimum kinetic energy the reactants should have in order to successfully react with each other and form new products. Physical chemists refer to this energy also as the *"activation energy barrier"*. Only those reactant particles (atoms or molecules) which have enough kinetic energy to "jump" over the E_a barrier will be converted to products. Temperature represents the amount of the kinetic energy of a system which all of us know as "heat".[1] The higher the kinetic energy, the higher the temperature and *vice versa*. Although heat is usually the type of energy exchanged in most chemical reactions, the E_a term could indeed indicate other types of energy such as photonic (light-related) and acoustic (sound-related). General examples of the latter two are photosynthetic reactions in plants, that use the energy from sunlight to make sugars from water and carbon dioxide, and ultrasound-driven chemical reactions.

3. **Solvent.** The type of solvent (or the medium in which a reaction is to take place) is important as a provider of the "right" environment to initiate a reaction and drive it to completion. As mentioned before, formation of molecules from atoms, or from other molecules for that matter, involve electronic interactions and exchanges. These electronic interactions and exchanges take place, again with some exceptions, through the mediacy of solvents. An analogy may be drawn by considering the transfer of electricity from power plants to your home. In this process electrons are transferred at almost the speed of light and through wires. The wires are, therefore, the media that bring you the "vital juice" on which our livelihood depends so critically these days. The same is true of chemical reactions, except in this case, solvents replace wires. Through solvents, electrons move and are exchanged among the reactants, and thus, new product molecules are formed. An appropriate solvent would be, therefore, required for any solution-phase reaction to commence, progress, and completes. For most biological reactions, including those leading to the formation and development of life, that solvent is called hydrogen oxide, a.k.a., water.
4. **Concentration.** Concentration, or the *number* of reactant particles per unit volume of a given chemical reaction, is important to initiate a reaction and drive it to completion. Obviously, the higher the number, the higher the concentration. The concentration parameter is important because it determines how frequently the reacting partners meet each other. And, all other requirements satisfied, the more frequently they meet, the more offspring they would produce. If you have only two microscopic particles suspended in a glass of water, the chances that they ever "see" each other are far less than if you had a

billion of each in the same glass. Nevertheless, extremely high concentrations also could have an antagonistic effect towards the rate and the extent of the reaction progress.

Now that we are a little bit more familiar with the nuts and bolts of chemical reactions, let's go back to the imaginary reaction which I offered to discuss at the end of Chapter 4: Let's just imagine that we have a bunch of atoms or molecules in our reaction vessel. And let me refer to them only as "particles" for simplicity and regardless of what type of atoms or molecules they are. If these particles are capable of chemically reacting with each other to form new particles, they would do it in a certain and well-defined fashion based on what we have learned about atomic and electronic structures and chemical bonds. Let's dissect this a little deeper and imagine that we have two different kinds of particles in our vessel, particle A and particle B, each with *its* specific electronic structure. Let's also assume that these particles are chemically reactive towards each other. Since both particles are in the same pot, the peripheral factors are the same for both. So, what could we expect to happen under these conditions? We have some reaction condition which regardless of what it is, is the same for *all* reactant particles. We also have two groups of particles, each with its own specific electronic structure, and thus, its own specific chemical properties, and which are mutually reactive. Therefore, what would happen is the formation of some product (or products, depending on the nature of reactants) with *determined* structures. The word "determined" in here means the product of this reaction would have its own chemical and physical characteristics which are the reflection of two variables: The properties of the reacting particles, and the nature of the peripheral conditions. A third and equally important meaning of "determined" is that should we be able to *recreate* the exact same experimental conditions (including the reactants) anywhere in the world, we should also be able to end up with the exact same results. And it should be to no surprise either: At least in this universe, natural processes, including chemical reactions, follow strict natural rules.[2] In fact, we may consider Nature to be a digital phenomenon. The outcome of any process within this universe could be assigned one of the two numbers, either a 1 (thumbs up, success, positive) or a 0 (thumbs down, failure, negative). Events either happen or they don't. And if they do happen, the exact same Events would recur should we be able to recreate the exact same conditions as before. And this should be true of all processes, from the simplest to the most complicated.

So, what about randomness and chaos? In this unimaginably vast Universe with such a large number of particles within, how could you *not* expect to have randomness, chance events, and thus chaos? Well, that is *"The"* question that this book is trying to ultimately answer and that *"Answer"* shall be elaborated upon in the last two chapters of the book, but since it's so (salivatingly) tempting, let's look at another hypothetical experiment as a warmer-upper:

Let's imagine this time you have 5 different types of particles in your reaction vessel, A, B, C, D, and E. All particles are in exactly the same number, and all are capable of reacting with each other, but they become unreactive after the first coupling. That way, every product of this reaction would be a diatomic molecule. And to be easy on our imaginations, let's assume that coupling of each two particles yields the same product regardless of the order of the coupling. That means, for example, product AB is the same as product BA, and so on. So, we put them all in the same reaction vessel, set up the suitable conditions, and switch it on. After however long the completion time is, we will have the following product combination in the reaction soup:

AB, AC, AD, AE, BC, BD, BE, CD, CE, and DE

[As a side note, I should also add that in this and any similar reaction, and under the same conditions, the number of possible pairs of products may be calculated from the following equation:

$$P = [n \cdot (n-1)]/2$$

where P is the number of possibilities and n is the number of particles.]

Now to test the degree of your companion's intelligence you may ask her "aside from their specific characteristics, what else is different between each product?" If she says "their quantities", she's smart and you should reward her in some nice way. Yes, although all reactant particles originally were equal quantities, the product particles would be made in different numbers. Although not necessarily, there should be different amounts of each product. There *could be* more AB than AD, less CD than DE, and so on. And the reason for this should be easy to see: The frequency of colliding each one of the five particles with others (to make products) *could be* not the same for all of them. If the A particles meet more Bs than they do Ds, naturally there will be more ABs than ADs. And the same holds for each and every other particle, and thus, the quantity of each single product could be (maybe not, but *could be*) different than those of others', varying from zero to a maximum which is limited to the total number of the initial reactant particles.

Now, if you repeated the very same experiment under exactly the same conditions only at a different time, one of three different outcomes could be the actual possibility:

1. All products form at equal quantities.
2. All products form at exactly the same ratios as in the first experiment.
3. All products form at new ratios that are different among themselves and different from those of the first experiment.

Although the first two situations would not be impossible, if we wanted to be totally honest with ourselves we should accept that scenario 3 should have a higher chance of occurrence. And to some, this conclusion may immediately point to a random, undetermined, and even chaotic nature of the world. Or putting it digitally, Determinism: 0, Freewill: 1.

Respectfully, I disagree, and I disagree based on the following logic:

1. Any two, or more, Events that are separated by either time or location, or both, shall be two, or more, separate Events.
2. No matter how carefully the setting up of two, or more, experiments, or any Event for that matter, is carried out, at microscopic (*i.e.*, atomic and molecular) levels, no two set-ups shall be 100% identical.
3. Logics 1 and 2 prove our inability to predict, with 100% accuracy, the outcome of any Event, and therefore the Future.
4. Logics 1-3 do not prove that the behavior of particles, within each section in time, is not according to a cause-and-effect history, and therefore, is not deterministic.

The easy translation of these logics is that our inability to *exactly* reproduce the initial conditions to repeat an Event, and therefore, to predict the future with 100% accuracy, should not mean that the World does not operate deterministically. We shall come back to this discussion in Chapter 12 with more details but for right now, let's continue our journey into our logic-based and logically created World.

NOTES

[1] Kinetic energy is really the "vibration" of macroscopic particles such as atoms and molecules. The higher the kinetic energy, the faster the vibration, and so the hotter the particles would be.

[2] The phrase "At least in this universe .." is used to acknowledge the "multiverse" or "parallel universes" hypotheses proposed by some physicists and based on some of the interpretations of quantum mechanics. According to these hypotheses, there may be more than one universe including the one we live in.

REFERENCES

1. Brown TL, *et al.*, *Chemistry – the Central Science*, Prentice Hall, 9th Ed, 2003, ISBN 0-13-066997-0.
2. Dougherty DA and Anslyn EV, *Modern Physical Organic Chemistry*, University Science Books, Sausalito, CA, USA, 2006, ISBN 9781891389313.

CHAPTER 7

The Feat

WHAT WE HAVE DISCUSSED SO far includes some basic knowledge about the fundamental aspects of our world and the science that applies equally effectively to both the "Living" and the "Non-Living".[1] Here in this chapter, though, we shift gears to a topic that applies to the former category, the domain of the Living. The rationale for adding this topic was two-fold: 1. To show how some special *arrangement* of atoms and molecules, or what some consider Non-Living, could now bring us to the world of the Living, and coupled with the material covered in the next chapter, 2. To lead our discussion to how those arrangements are the determining factors in our decision-making processes. And, of course, we need not be reminded about the close relationship between the ability of decision-making and our possession of Freewill. A combination of the two facts shown in 1 and 2, above, and the mechanisms through which the rest of our Universe operates, should then be able to provide us with an *overall theory* capable of describing the deterministic nature of the World.

    I am not shy about saying that I got misty-eyed when I first learned how the genetic system worked. I was absolutely amazed about so much sophistication, so much mastery, and so much intelligence that was implied in this system all put together by but a small group of small atoms! And by "genetic system" I do not mean only ours but those too of other animals, plants, fungi, even that of a seemingly lowly bacterium. Yes, bacterium, the creature whose single cell doesn't even have a nucleus, flashes out such a masterpiece that dazes the mental eyes of anyone who dares looking deeply into it.

Not many people need be reminded that the genetic machinery of any reproducing organism is, in fact, the blueprint of not only the physical, but as we shall see in the next chapter, the incorporeal *"self"* of that organism all written in chemical language (*1*). There are two very interesting features associated with this system:

1. The language of genetics is universal, that is, it is written with basically the same alphabet for all organisms.
2. The language uses only five chemical elements as its *"atomic alphabet"*. These elements are hydrogen (H), carbon (C), nitrogen (N), oxygen (O), and phosphorus (P).[2]

The feat of genetics started many, many years ago, by the coming together of the *"atomic letters"* of the genetic language, the H, C, N, O, and P atoms, to form the *"words"* that the language is written in. And that's where the miracle begins: Billions and billions of pieces of information, written with only five letters!

There are three different types of "words" in this language but let's, for the sake of simplicity, call these words by their scientific name, "molecules" (you may recall from Chapter 3 that molecules are formed when two or more atoms bond together). Chemically speaking, these three types of molecules operating within the genome, belong to the chemical super families of phosphates, carbohydrates (the chemical name for sugars), and heterocycles (called bases in the genetic jargon), all made from the five elements shown above. And to be genetically functional, phosphates, sugars, and bases teamed up in groups of three, with one member coming from each family: One phosphate, one sugar, and one base. Each of these triplet combinations is called a *nucleotide*. The prefix *"nucleo"* comes from the fact that in eukaryotic cells (cells possessing nuclei like our cells) the main genetic machinery is contained in, and operated from, the cell nucleus (see below). While the chemical structure of the sugar and phosphate parts are the same across the board, there are five different compounds in the base group, which enter the nucleotides (the genetic words) one at a time. These five bases are called adenine (abbreviated as A), cytosine (C), guanine (G), thymine (T), and uracil (U), and are made of either one (cytosine, thymine, and uracil) or two (adenine and guanine) cyclic (or ring) structures. The ring sections are made from the binding together of carbon and nitrogen atoms. Still note that, despite the structural diversities of these five bases, all of them are made with different combinations of carbon, hydrogen, nitrogen, and oxygen atoms, that is, four of the five atomic letters mentioned above. The generic name for the one-ring structures is "pyrimidine" and that of the two-ring systems is "purine". As a representative example, the structure of a nucleotide is shown in Figure 1. Here, the part with a "P" in the center is the phosphate segment, the ring structure in the middle containing an oxygen (O) is the sugar part (a form of ribose in this case), and the scary-looking N-containing double-ring structure to the right is the base (in this case a purine called adenine, A). Since the base is an adenine and the sugar is a deoxyribose (one of the members of the carbohydrate super family), this nucleotide is called an *"adenine deoxyribonucleotide"*.

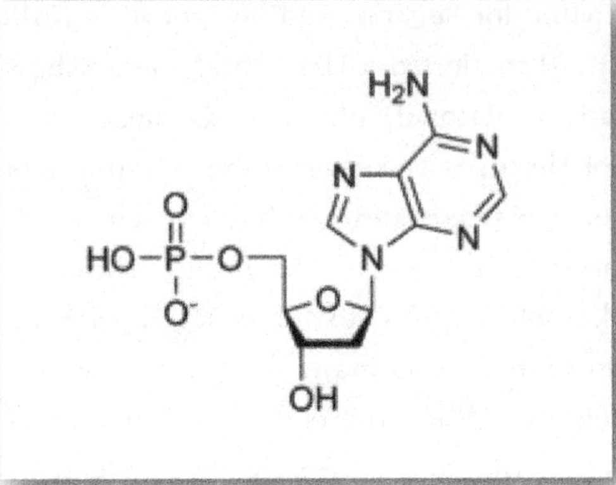

Figure 1. Representative structure of a nucleotide: adenine deoxyribonucleotide.

Ok, I know, I said five atoms make these structures, so where is the fifth one, carbons, in Figure 1? You're right, but let me tell you that they're there, only not shown, and here's why: Despite their reputation as being difficult, picky, and sometimes grumpy-faced people, chemists are really kind and thoughtful people too who sometime do things to make life a bit easier for you. Like in this, and other organic chemical structures, chemists decided to show carbon atoms (C's), and the hydrogens attached to them, with just simple-looking angles (like > or ≥). You may agree with them once you realize that how complicated the look of the structure of Figure 1 would become if you replaced all those angles with C's. And it's not the whole mess either. Depending on its structural location, you have to attach one or two hydrogens (H's) to each carbon too. Just picture this structure in which each line angle is replaced with either an H-C-H or a C-H. I am sure now you could easily appreciate the simplification that this angles-for-carbons convention brings about in representing organic chemical structures.

So, there you are, now you know all (!) the secrets of how to interpret a chemical structure like our adenine deoxyribonucleotide (DRN) of Figure 1.

The design of this structure is not accidental or for the looks of it, by the way. Every single piece is there for a reason: The phosphate function is for connecting these molecules to other DRN's as well as for inducing better water solubility and metabolic advantages. The phosphate segments work as "bridges" that connect each DRN unit to other DRNs in the chains of DNA molecules as we shall see later. The sugar moieties contribute to the overall water solubility of the molecules too, as the base units (A, T, C, G, and U) have poor water solubility. For most biomolecules, poor solubility in water, the solvent of life, jeopardizes their functions and their utilization by the cells, tissues, and organisms.

So how do these molecules work in the genome? How do these "chemical words" communicate with each other, with the parent generation, and then with the progeny in the reproducing organisms?

During the recent years (with the writing time of this manuscript as the reference) the acronym "DNA" has been really in vogue. Even people who do not know where it comes from and what it exactly does, use it as if everybody is a geneticist! ".. cars made by this automaker have Performance in their DNA .." exclaims the salesman with a proud face. Or ".. serving the people of this country as best as I can is in the DNA of my future strategies .." announces this disparate public office candidate, who if lost, has to explain why to his investors, and even worse, to his wife!

Rhetorical usages aside, the three letters of the acronym stand for "DeoxyriboNucleic Acid" (capitalizations are for illustration only). Nucleic acids (or really ribonucleic acids) were first isolated and discovered by physiological chemist Friedrich Miescher (1844-1895) and were named as such because they were first found in cells nuclei (thus the adjective "nucleic"). The word "acid" came from the fact that they contained phosphate groups, a derivative of phosphoric acid, and "ribo" because the molecules contained the sugar ribose.

Structurally, DNA consists of two strands of polynucleotides (poly = many), a long chain of head-to-tail-connected nucleotides, each with a chemical structure similar to the one shown in Figure 1 except with different bases. The bases of the DNA are A, C, G, and T only (U is used somewhere else as discussed later). A crude and rough representation of a typical single strand may be shown as in Figure 2:

$$\ldots [\text{O-P(O)}_2\text{-O-}sugar\text{-}\mathbf{A}\text{-O-P(O)}_2\text{-O-}sugar\text{-}\mathbf{C}\text{-O-P(O)}_2\text{-O-}sugar\text{-}\mathbf{G}\text{- O-P(O)}_2\text{-O-}sugar\text{-}\mathbf{T}\text{-}]_n \ldots$$

Figure 2. The general representation of a polynucleotide chain. *n* is any non-zero integer depending on the length of the strand. The O-P(O)$_2$-O segments denote the phosphate groups.

One of the beauties, and at the same time key features, of these molecules is the mutual and specific affinities between A and T, and between C and G bases (2). When in close proximity, and adenine (A's) binds to a thymine (T's) while a cytosine (C's) binds to a guanine (G's) through hydrogen bond formation (Chapter 4). It should be reemphasized that these bindings are mutual and structure-specific. These are schematically shown in Figure 3.

Figure 3. Binding between A and T (A…T) and C and G (C…G) bases in DNA to form base pairs. Dotted lines indicate hydrogen bonds. Wavy lines indicate the sugar and phosphate segments that are omitted for simplicity.

Based on the specificity of these bindings, each base is called "*complementary*" to the one it binds to. Thus, A is complementary to T (and *vice versa*) and C is complementary to G (and *vice versa*). By the same token, a chain (or strand) of polynucleotide may be complementary to another strand if the second one has a matching set of complementary bases that are strung in the right order. The complementary strand to the one shown in Figure 2 is shown in Figure 4 below:

$$... [\text{O-P(O)}_2\text{-O-}sugar\text{-T-O-P(O)}_2\text{-O-}sugar\text{-G-O-}$$
$$\text{P(O)}_2\text{-O-}sugar\text{-C- O-P(O)}_2\text{-O-}sugar\text{-A-}]_n ...$$

Figure 4. The complementary strand to the strand of Figure 2.

And when I called the complementary features of the DNA bases a "beauty", it's because of these features (among others): The "complementarity" means if you dissolved ten each of the two single-strand polynucleotide molecules of Figures 2 and Figure 4 in buffered water, they would *automatically* form ten double-stranded (DS) DNA molecules. These DS molecules sort of look like ladders whose rungs are the hydrogen bonds between each base pair (Hint: Look at Figure 3 again).

THE DOUBLE HELIX STRUCTURE

You might have noticed that, in our world, environment, daily life, *etc.*, usually the more delicate, the more sensitive, and the more complicated the job or output of a system is, the more sophisticated and organized the physical structure of that system needs to be. At a microscopic level, consider the structure of even the simplest of all chemical elements, the hydrogen atom. One proton in the center with an orbiting electron around it. As long as the electron in this system is defined by, and obeys, the four specific quantum numbers (discussed in Chapter 3), the atom could continue to survive. Once any of these is violated, the atom would no longer be. In other words, It has to be so to be so. The hydrogen atom *is* the simplest of elements in the Periodic Table but simplicity is a relative term. When looked deeply into its physics and mathematics, we find the orbital shape of its simply-single electron is to be defined by a not-so-simple Schrödinger Wave Equation (3). It will then be easy to extrapolate this example to larger atoms to see, for example, that gold has an atomic structure millions of times more complicated than hydrogen's, and as such, it has chemical and mechanical characteristics that put it in the rank of "Precious Metals". Gold's "rareness" is directly related to nothing but its complicated and specific atomic structure and electronic configuration.

At a macroscopic level, the same is true of our own human world too. A business has to be organized and well-structured to be profitable, and therefore, survivable. And why do you think the fundamental principle in any sports team is strict discipline? Why players have to eat, sleep, and manage themselves in certain ways for their team to be a winner? I guess the answers are more than obvious to all of us: Well-organized and well-disciplined systems have more efficiency and chance of survival than those that are not.

So, let's not be too surprised if we found very specialized types of structures for the double-stranded polynucleotides, one form of which being the DNA molecule. After all, what in the world could be more sensitive, important, complicated, and sophisticated than replicating (and therefore, continuing) generations of different organisms? Is it not like a miracle that after a joyful union we produce someone like ourselves who (usually) could do exactly the same things as we do and sometimes even better, and all that from a couple of tiny, even incomplete cells? If your answers to these two questions (two just to keep it simple, many more could've been asked) were *"not many things"* and *"it definitely is*", respectively, then you may be interested in knowing how the DNA looks like (if you don't already, of course).

The very nature of the molecule, the involved chemical bonds, the size, order, and properties of the participating atoms, and the amount of the attractive forces among them, dictate the twisting of the ladder-shaped molecule of the double-stranded DNA into a helical conformation. Going back to our ladder example, imagine you are holding the two ends of a small rubbery-soft ladder by both of your hands and gently twist them in opposite directions. That would make a crude model of the DNA molecule. Even a better idea is to look at Figure 5 which shows a cartoon representation of the DNA double helix. The phosphate and sugar segments comprise the double helix backbones (the side poles of the ladder) and the base residues with their hydrogen bonds connecting each pair of them make the rungs of the ladder.

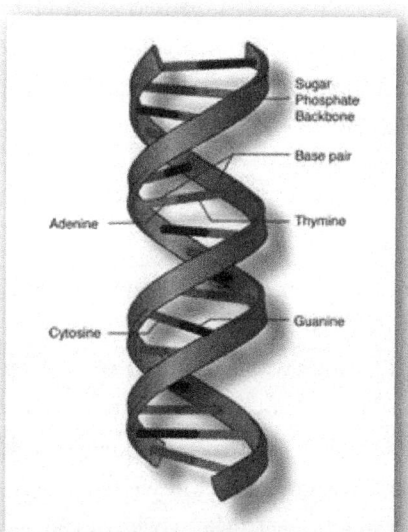

Figure 5. Schematic representation of the DNA double helix. The side-ribbons denote the sugar-phosphate segments bridged by the base pairs (A-T and C-G) and their connecting hydrogen bonds. Figure credit.[3]

There is no need to emphasize too much on the fact that the success of these molecules is in their structures. It is the design of these structures that allows the other participants of the feat of heredity come into play as we shall see later. Please keep in mind that discussing the reasons that caused the DNA and other biomolecules come into existence is not within the scope of this book. Rather, it is the *relationship* between the *arrangements* of the atoms (*i.e.*, the atomic configurations) and *what happens as a result*, which I would like to focus on and to ultimately arrive at the final conclusions of these discussions. As you read through this book, just keep one thing in the front row of your memory cells: This book is trying to prove that things, both non-living and living (as per the conventional definitions) have their natures, characteristics, and properties, based on the specific ways that their atoms have come together.[1] In my opinion, it is this arrangement, and this arrangement only, that determines the *nature* and *properties of* any "Thing" at all and it is the nature and properties of those Things (and I mean *all* Things) that determined what has happened, and will determine what will happen, in the future.

GENES

I am pretty sure you expected this coming. After all, what is the next topic after a DNA discussion? Genes, of course. After "DNA", "gene" is the other related famous word. In fact, were it up to me, I would've called them "genies" instead of genes, for they are really wonder-doers. So marvelous is what they do that it makes them kind of scary even. Although to be fair, I should also acknowledge the contribution of other amazing molecular machines to the works of the genetic system.

Genes are relatively large blocks (or better said, strings) of DNA and are the molecular units of heredity (*1*). They contain, and pass on from one generation to the next, the hereditary information of biologically active organisms. And this information determines what a given organism is, which is for example, how my daughter could tell me from her cats. In the case of humans, genes determine if they have dark or blond hair, black or blue eyes, are tall or short, could drink milk or are lactose-intolerant, have a love for music or hate math, have a cool or hot temper, and millions of other physical and psychological traits and just about anything you could think of that makes us "Us". Arguments may be thrown in by some that we are not 100% nature and that there is a "nurture" factor too which plays a role in who we are. Again, I will have to disagree. But why I disagree, will be discussed in the last two chapters of this book. For right now, let's just focus on genes.

As mentioned above, genes are segments (or *loci*) of long strings of DNA with the latter being parts of another highly organized structure called a chromosome. Chromosomes are contained inside of the nucleus of eukaryotic (or nucleus-possessing) cells. In prokaryotes (or cells without nuclei like bacteria) chromosomes are immersed freely in the cells' cytoplasm.

Volumes could be written on the structure and mechanism of action of genes, chromosomes, and the accompanying "helper hand" proteins (called enzymes) that collectively constitute the machinery of the heredity and reproduction processes, but for our current discussion, let's just suffice by briefly mentioning the highlights of the system.

So, what does it mean when we say DNA is responsible for transferring the genetic information from parents to the offspring, or simply put, what do genes do? The short answer is: They copy proteins. And proteins agent the formation of other molecules, that in turn, bring about the formation of a living organism.

GENE EXPRESSION

Most probably you have seen the blueprint of your (or somebody else's) house produced by an architect or an engineer. Unless you have prior training or experience, those lines, dots, and numbers on a building plan really don't mean much even if you knew it was supposed to be a house when fully executed. Not too long ago, I asked my programmer to resize the logo of my company so I could fit it into a business card format. After exchanging a few emails with the logo's "jpeg" file going back and forth, he finally ran out of patience and said ".. look I'll send you a zip file containing different versions of your logo. Take whichever you choose to your printer and tell them to use it on the biz card." When I opened the files, I saw there were three files, Adobe, PNG, and JPEG, which after opening, showed the logo. But there was one of them, called "EPS" file, that contained nothing but words, signs, and numbers. Nothing even remotely resembling my company logo. Not being in the field, I had never seen that type of conversion but on inquiry, it turned out that it actually was the logo except in a different language. Once translated (decoded) those words, signs, and numbers would have produced the logo picture in one piece.

Such is the story of the genetic codes, decoded into the production of proteins, a process which is executed by the cells' protein-making machinery. This translation of the genetic code to production of proteins is termed *"gene expression"*. In this marvelous process, the genetic code, written in chemistry language, is decoded into tangible molecules of proteins, or Nature's building machines (4). These proteins would in turn manufacture other types of molecules like lipids (or fats), carbohydrates (or sugars), *etc.*, that collectively make up the whole of an organism's body. The overall outcome: Reproduction of the organism!

Gene expression is carried out in two main steps: Transcription and translation. I discuss these two processes here very concisely and only to the extent that serves the purposes of this book. All I want to relay to you here is that, just like any other natural process in our world, reproduction (and therefore propagation of life) is a strictly controlled and molecule-based event which obeys the solid and unchangeable physical laws of Nature.

Transcription. Transcription is a process in which the genetic information contained in DNA is copied (or transcribed) into another molecule called messenger RNA (mRNA), which in turn, would deliver that information to another site for the synthesis of a new but exact copy of the original DNA molecule (5). The process is described below but for right now remember that at the beginning of this chapter I mentioned something about the complementarity aspect of the DNA bases (see Figures 2-4). As a refresher, bases A and T specifically pair up with each other by forming hydrogen bonds. The same is true of C and G which pair up together. Under normal conditions, the pairings would not occur between A and C or G, and between T and C or G. What I did not mention there was that there is another type of poly nucleotide albeit not as famous as DNA among the non-science folks. This other equally important nucleic acid is called RNA (for RiboNucleic Acid) which also plays a key role in genetic processes. You may consider RNA as still a DNA with two differences: 1. It has an extra hydroxyl (OH) group on the sugar (ribose) ring of its nucleotide units, and 2. Instead of thymine (T) that is present in DNA, it has another structurally related base called uracil (U, shown in Figure 6). And just like T, U has a complementary affinity for A (similar to the ones shown in Figure 3).

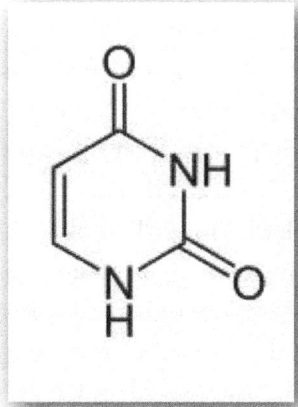

Figure 6. Chemical structure of uracil (U).

To summarize, we have two kinds of polynucleotide nucleic acids, DNA and RNA. Compared to DNA, RNA has one extra OH group in its ribose sugar units and it has uracil instead of the thymine of DNA. Complementary base pairing in DNA occurs as A-to-T and C-to-G whereas in RNA it's A-to-U and C-to-G.

The other point I wanted to bring to your attention is the function of specialized proteins called *"enzymes"* that play key roles in biological reactions in general and in genetic processes in particular. If the nucleic acids could be compared to the software of computers because they contain and transfer information (in this case the genetic information), one may consider enzymes the "hardware" of genetically conducted operations. As discussed in Chapter 5, proteins may have well-defined and function-related tertiary and quaternary structures. As enzymes, they could work as molecular vessels in which other molecules are assembled or disassembled. They may also operate as ion-carriers, chemical reaction accelerators, and molecular organizers, to name a few of their functions. That's why proteins are informally called Nature's chemical workhorses.

Like many other biological processes, DNA (or in a wider view, the gene) transcription is cranked up, and carried out, by a bunch of enzymes. The major one is called RNA polymerase (here abbreviated as RPase). RPase chemically *recognizes*, and binds to, specific regions of the DNA called *"promoters"*. Chemical "recognition" is done in Nature all the time between proteins and other molecules including other proteins. All it takes is a protein (in this case RPase) whose structure is evolved to contain cavities with topological features matching a certain atom or molecule (in this case the promoter region of a DNA). You may think of it as a lock-and-key or a mold-and-cast duo. Once bound to the DNA promoter, the RPase begins to unwind the DNA double helix (shown in Figure 5). In molecular biology, this step is called *"initiation"*. In the next step, called elongation, RPase uses the necessary building blocks to *"transcribe"* (or copy) the gene (which is structurally a DNA). The "copy" would not be another DNA though. Rather, it's a new RNA for reasons having to do with molecular bond stabilities, another testament to Nature's intelligence and "wit". Nature deposits the information in a molecule that is not easily decomposed or digested by other enzymes and molecules, as RNA is chemically more stable than DNA. Nature does this to keep the copied information safe. The building blocks of RNA synthesis would be phosphates, ribose, and bases, just like those of its DNA cousins. Since the newly synthesized strand (called the transcript) is going to be an RNA, the building block bases are A, U, C, and G where U has replaced T of the template DNA. The transcription process is done off of only one of the two unwound strands of the original DNA called the *"template strand"*. The other strand (which is not copied) is called a *"coding strand"*. Remember what I said about the specific and complementary base paring? Good! The RPase uses this property of the nucleic bases to string the said building blocks in the phosphate-sugar-base order in such a way that each A, T, C, and G base on the template strand is paired up, respectively, with a U, A, G, and C base on the new RNA strand. Now if you showed this RNA to anyone with a limited knowledge about the complementary base pairing and ask him what the structure of the original DNA strand off of which this RNA was transcribed had been, he should be able to give you the exact structure. And if you decided to be a pain in the ear, you could next ask him about the structure of the *other* strand of the original DNA double helix (that is the coding strand). If the buddy has paid enough attention to the base pairing discussion, he should be able to easily deny you the pleasure and give you the correct structure: It is the same as that of the new RNA except you have T's instead of U's. The single strand of the transcribed RNA contains not only the complete genetic information contained in the DNA strand that it was directly copied from, but it also has the information about the other strand of the original DNA double helix. Therefore, by looking at any RNA molecule you'd be able to deduce the structures of both strands of the original piece of DNA double helix, that is, the gene. Accordingly, the transcribed RNA thus produced is called a messenger RNA (mRNA) because, as we shall see later, it carries and delivers the genetic information (the message) of the individual organism it was produced from. Such is the beauty and wisdom of Nature!

Finally, in the last step of transcription, called *"termination"*, the synthesis of the mRNA comes to a halt. I said earlier that genes are long DNA strands made of phosphate, sugar, and base (A, T, C, G) moieties. At the end of each gene, there are regions in which series of G..C base pairs are followed by series of A..T base pairs. These are molecular stop signs through which the gene "commands" the elongation of the mRNA to stop, the mRNA-DNA complex to dissociate, the PRase to release the parent DNA, and the parent DNA to rewind back into its original double helical configuration. It is all chemistry. Chemical language based on molecular recognition. Chemtalk at its best, ... and nothing supernatural!

Thus, a new copy of the gene, the mRNA, is made to relay the message of the *"Grand Master"*, the genome, to the extra-nuclear machinery of the cell to make a new copy of the whole organism; the organism that could be you, your pet, your favorite flower in your backyard, or the mosquito that drives you nuts every time you dare to caress that flower.

Before I go into the description of the next step (the translation), I have to tell you about another smart "molecular trick" that genes play to promote themselves. And it is part of the answer to this question: "How genes manage to make proteins?" After all, genes are a totally different kind of molecules than proteins from a chemistry point of view. As a refresher, proteins are chains of amino acids (see Chapter 5) while genes are chains of nucleotides (see Figure 1). So, what kind of "interface" is used to translate genes into proteins?

Codons and anticodons. The answers to that question are *"codons"* and *"anticodons"*, the specific triplet combinations of the four bases A, U, C, and G on the mRNA strand. After a series of absolutely elegant experiments in 1961, Francis Crick (1916-2004) and his colleagues found out that for each amino acid used in the synthesis of natural proteins, there is at least one 3-base combination in mRNA molecules (6). They called these triple combinations "codons". And with the exception of the amino acids methionine and tryptophan, there are more than one codon for every amino acid. For example, the codons for the amino acid alanine are "GCU", "GCC", "GCA", and "GCG". This means that anytime the genetically operated protein-making machinery of the cells runs into a "GCU" combination (or any one of this series), on the mRNA, one molecule of alanine is added into the protein molecule that is under construction. We will see this in the following section. Remember there are 22 proteinogenic (protein-making) amino acids. Of these, 20 are coded for in the genomes of all species, each with its own codon(s). The other two are produced only in non-eukaryotic cells such as bacteria and archea (microbes belonging to the domain of prokaryotes or single-celled organisms) (7, *8*, 9).

The opposite of codons, that is, their complementary triple nucleotides (see Figure 3 of this chapter and the related discussion), are called *"anticodons"*. Codons and their complementary anticodons pair up with each other through hydrogen bonds, as described for DNA complementary base pairing, and are therefore capable of *"reading"* each other. Furthermore, all the amino acid codons are, by convention, referred to as *"sense"* codons. So, does this mean that there are such things as *"nonsense"* codons? Yes, these are also triplet nucleotides that do not (always) encode for amino acids but play another important role: They tell the system when to stop making proteins. How do they stop the protein-making process? Easy, because they don't encode for any amino acid so they can't make any *"sense"*!

Ribosomal and transfer RNAs. When I talked about RNA and mRNA in the last section, I did not tell you that there were two additional types of RNA too. One is called ribosomal RNA (rRNA) and the other transfer RNA (tRNA). Ribosomal RNA is part of a large molecule called ribosome which is composed of RNAs and proteins and is literally the protein manufacturing site and machinery of a cell. To make it short and sweet, we don't want to go into a detailed description of ribosomes, just remember that it has three subunits denoted A, P, and E. We'll find out what these subunits are for in a few lines below.

The third RNA molecule, tRNA, is in charge of carrying and delivering (*i.e.*, transferring) amino acids, the building blocks of proteins, to the protein factory site (the ribosome) during the protein synthesis step. Think of tRNA as a string of nucleotides usually 76 to 90 nucleotides long. At one end, it carries the specific amino acid it is supposed to transfer and deliver to the protein making site, and at the other it contains the anticodon for that same amino acid. So, in the alanine example of the previous section, the corresponding tRNA is attached to one of the alanine anticodon combinations CGA, CGG, CGU, or CGC (the anticodons for GCU, GCC, GCA, GCG alanine codons- Note the complementarity between bases) at one end, and to one molecule of alanine at the other. Attachment of amino acids to tRNAs is done by specialized enzymes called *"activating enzymes"* (chemical name: aminoacyl-tRNA synthetase). To add to the awe, the structures of these activating enzymes (which are themselves proteins) are such that each one enzyme is capable of pairing one anticodon (or in some cases more) to *one and only one* kind of amino acid. So, for each of the 20 natural amino acids, there is only one specific activating enzyme.

Now that we have an idea as to what codons, anticodons, and the three types of RNA are, I want you to keep in mind one more thing too. That codons are triple-nucleotide segments comprising the mRNA molecules while anticodons are triple-nucleotide segments in tRNA molecules. And while there are several different copies of codons along the mRNA molecules, there is only one copy of each anticodon per molecule of tRNA.

Ok, now while trying to remember all these let's move to the next section to see how the Symphony is played:

Translation. Translation is the last gene-mediated step of protein synthesis in which the three main players, ribosome, mRNA, and tRNA participate *(10)*. As mentioned above, this process takes place in a protein-making factory called the ribosome.[4] Ribosome consists of one small and one large subunit. The large subunit contains three sites within it, that are, sites A, P, and E. I shall tell you what they are for shortly. After the mRNA is transcribed off of a DNA (the gene) exits the nuclear compartment into the cytoplasm of the cell, specialized proteins called *"initiation factors"* pick it up and carry it over to the small subunit of the ribosome. At the beginning of every mRNA molecule is a *"start codon"*, usually AUG (remember codons and anticodons were triplet combos of nucleotides) which commands the *"start"* of the protein synthesis process (in other words, AUG and other start codons are "molecular triggers" that signal the start of protein synthesis). Then another initiation factor picks up a molecule of tRNA and carries it over to the same small subunit of the ribosome. Remember from above that tRNAs are carriers of amino acids and also contain anticodons at the end of their molecules. The first (or the *"start"*) tRNA has the trigger anticodon for AUG of the mRNA and therefore binds to this codon in the small ribosomal subunit. Think of the mRNA as a single tape of a zipper (as opposed to when you have a whole zipper with two tapes that come together). The combination of each three teeth on this tape is one codon (such as ACG, UGA, *etc.*). In contrast, the tRNA may be pictured as a single zipper tape too, except that none but three of its teeth fit their complementary teeth of the other zipper tape, or the mRNA. This triple combination is the anticodon. And remember, for this anticodon there is one and only one amino acid located at the other end of the tRNA. Although there are 20 standard amino acids in natural, genetically coded proteins, there are a mixture of 64 tRNAs (each with a different anticodon) in the genetic coding system. The reason is in some cases, the same amino acids is coded with more than one codon-anticodon pair.

When brought together in the small subunit of the ribosome, (and using the zipper model) the three teeth of the methionine-tRNA-UAC zipper lock into the three AUG teeth of the mRNA and the start of the protein synthesis process is signaled. The combination of the small ribosomal subunit, tRNA, and mRNA is called the *"initiation complex"*. When it is formed, the whole complex would attach to the large subunit of ribosome in such a way that the tRNA-mRNA couple sits in the "P" (for "Peptidyl") site of the large subunit. In this exact position, the next codon of the mRNA (the next three teeth of the single zipper tape) would be exposed at the "A" (for "Acyl") site of the large subunit. The codon is immediately recognized by its complementary anticodon on another molecule of tRNA which also carries the encoded amino acid at its other end. Once there, the two amino acids (the one in site P carried in by the first tRNA and the one brought in by the second tRNA) are coupled together to form a peptide bond (the bond that holds amino acid molecules together in a protein as discussed in Chapter 5), the first amino acid (the one sitting in the P-site) is released from its tRNA, the tRNA minus its amino acid moves one site over into the "E" site (for "Exit") and from there permanently leaves the factory. This cycle is repeated for as many times as written in the mRNA code, leading to the production of a chain of amino acids, also known as "proteins". These proteins could now be your skin, muscle, hair, your pet's tongue, your grandma's finger nail, or your favorite milk shake. It all depends on its primary structure, the kind and order of binding together of its building block amino acids (Chapter 5).

WHAT WAS THIS ALL FOR?

That's a legitimate question you have the right to ask. Why did we talk about what nucleotides, DNA, RNA, and genes are, and why did we bother discussing what these molecules do in living organisms' cells? And I know that no matter how much I try to write it in a simple language so it be easy to grasp, it is the nature of some parts of science that makes the discussion not too easy (and believe me, writing them in an easy language is no easy task). There are three reasons for including this chapter in this book (the first of which is not the main one, albeit an important one): First, to provide some introductory and basic information for those readers who had never read about how the genetic system works. Who knows, it may come handy sometime too. These days, we hear a lot about genes and DNA so we may as well have a little background about them. Second, to demonstrate, and emphasize on, the continuation of the systematic progression of *Existence* at large, from the simple atom of hydrogen to the extremely complex organisms, from microscopic to macroscopic, all the while pointing to an uninterrupted connectivity among all components of the Universe, which may be a firm evidence for a cause-and-effect mechanism in natural processes. When we reach towards the last chapters of this book, it will become more obvious why this connectivity and the cause-and-effect phenomenon should be appreciated. And the third reason is to provide a basis for the discussion on the universal link between human consciousness and the spontaneous, independent, and stepwise flow of Existence, a subset of which we call *"Life"*. This last reason, of course, is because this book is being written by a human for other humans. Maybe if I were a computer that could write independently and on its own abilities, I would've written this chapter about how computers were made and what parts were needed and played roles in their manufacture and functions. As humans though, it may be useful to show how we come to *be* and how our *being* is connected to the rest of the World which we are only a subset of. The interesting point is that, even if I were that "author computer", the story of my and other computers' lives which I was writing about, would still show the same pattern of connectivity and cause-and-effect phenomena. As long as things are contained in this Universe, the take-home messages of all stories remain the same as long as they could be intellectually realized.

The information covered in this chapter demonstrates another step of the many steps involved in the formation of a special type of polyatomics known as *"The Living"*, those collections of atoms, which among some other functions, have the ability of copying themselves. And this "copying" is done by a bunch of highly organized and logic-driven chemical reactions and molecules. Furthermore, these reactions are all quality-driven under given ambient conditions, meaning the route from atom A (*e.g.*, phosphorous) to compound B (*e.g.*, phosphoric acid) to compound Z (*e.g.*, DNA) is determined by the chemical qualities (or properties) of all the atoms involved, those that are directly involved in chemical reactions and those that form the reaction vessel, a.k.a., the Environment.

Notes

[1] I use the words "Living" and "Non-living" separately here only to keep things simple. My own interpretation of these words is somewhat different in that, to me (and perhaps to those we call Panbioists) there is no Non-living thing in this world, and thus, all is Living. But that is a separate story which I would like to save for another time.

[2] Remember that at the time of this writing there are 112 chemical elements. Five is only less than 4.5% of them.

[3] Credit for Figure 5: This figure is courtesy of National Human Genome Research Institute's Talking Glossary (http://www.genome.gov/glossary).

[4] In prokaryotic cells (such as bacteria) which have no nucleus, the protein building process takes place all in one compartment, the main cytoplasmic body of the cell. In eukaryotes, after the transcription of the mRNA which contains the genetic code of the parent DNA in the parent cell's nucleus, the mRNA exits the nucleus through the pores of the nuclear envelope and into the cell's cytoplasm. Whatever the type of the cell (prokaryote or eukaryote) though, the fundamental mechanism is the same.

REFERENCES

1. Help Me Understand Genetics, *Genetics Home Reference*, https://ghr.nlm.nih.gov, 2017.
2. Berg J, Tymoczko J, Stryer L, *Biochemistry*, W. H. Freeman and Company, 2002, ISBN 0-7167-4955-6.
3. Schrödinger E, Die gegenwärtige Situation in der Quantenmechanik (German: "The Present Situation in Quantum Mechanics"), *Naturwissenschaften*, 23 (48): 807–812, 1935. DOI: 10.1007/BF01491891
4. Berk V, Cate JH, Insights into Protein Biosynthesis from Structures of Bacterial Ribosomes, *Curr Opin Struct Biol*, 17 (3): 302–309, 2007.
5. Clancy S, DNA Transcription, *Nature Ed*, 1(1): 41, 2008.
6. Crick F, The Genetic Code, In: *What Mad Pursuit: A Personal View of Scientific Discovery*, Basic Books, New York, pp. 89–101, 1988, ISBN 0-465-09138-5.
7. Jakubke H-D and Sewald N, Amino Acids, *Peptides from A to Z: A Concise Encyclopedia*, Wiley-VCH, 2008, ISBN: 9783527621170.
8. Wagner I and Musso H, New Naturally Occurring Amino Acids, *Angew Chem Int Ed Eng*, 22 (11): 816–828, 1983. DOI: 10.1002/anie.198308161
9. Hertweck C, Biosynthesis and Charging of Pyrrolysine, the 22nd Genetically Encoded Amino Acid, *Ang Chem Int Ed Eng*, 50 (41): 9540–9541, 2011.
10. Clancy S, Translation: DNA to mRNA to Protein, *Nature Ed*, 1 (1): 101, 2008.

CHAPTER 8

Structure-Function Relationships

—⋙—

SOMETIMES USEFUL THINGS ARE NOT important and other times important things are not useful but the subject of *"Quantitative Structure-Activity Relationship (QSAR)"* is both important *and* useful (*1*). This is a topic taught in some graduate chemistry and medicinal chemistry courses where the students learn how the arrangement of atoms in a molecule (or the molecular structure) determines the overall properties and chemical behavior of that molecule towards other molecules. The reason that QSAR is important and useful is that it could provide guidance to the design, and eventual production of, almost every kind of compound we use in our daily lives: Pharmaceuticals, food-related items, clothing material, pest control agents, agricultural compounds, *etc.*

The recent systematic studies of QSAR began more than a century ago when Alexander Crum-Brown (1838-1922) and Thomas Fraser (1841-1920) proposed that the physiological properties of compounds were a function of their molecular structure, although I am sure many other scientists had come to the same conclusion (it is the nature of scientific research that usually the early outspeaker gets the worm of fame).[1]

The foundation of QSAR is based on two premises: First, atoms acquire a new character when they become part of a molecule (as opposed to being free atoms), and second, the new character of the individual bonded atoms interact all over the molecule to produce an overall *"molecular property"*. As such, there is a correlation between molecular structure and molecular activity. QSAR is the science of figuring out, analyzing, quantifying, interpreting, and predicting these correlations by putting together mathematical molecular models and testing them against experimental data. The goal of this chapter is not teaching a QSAR course, but simply to demonstrate the significance of the relationship between the structure of a system (in general) and *what* that system would be capable of doing.

Take as an example the humble but wondrous drug, aspirin (chemical name: acetyl salicylic acid). Salicylate medications have been known to humans since about 2000 BCE and are derivatives of salicylic acid which is extracted from the barks of the willow tree and some other plants. It was not until 1853 that the French chemist, Charles Frédéric Gerhardt (1816-1856), changed the molecular structure of salicylic acid through chemical modification. Gerhardt's modification was done by connecting one of the oxygen atoms of salicylic acid to acetic acid (the active ingredient of vinegar) at a 1-to-1 molecular ratio and in a process known in chemistry as esterification. Forty-four years later in 1897, scientists at the German chemical and pharmaceutical company, Bayer, discovered that Gerhardt's compound had the same pharmacological benefits as salicylates except it was systemically less irritating, and thus, more tolerable. They quickly formulated the compound as an analgesic and antipyretic drug and marketed it worldwide as Aspirin. The rest is history (or more history) but this was a simple example of how even a simple change in molecular structure, an esterification in this case, of an otherwise irritating molecule made it milder, and therefore, more tolerable, hence more useful, and thence, a commodity!

The science of QSAR may be considered a specific subsection of a more general chapter, the structure-function relationship (SFR) which indicates how the properties of any system, in a very general sense, are functions of the micro- and/or macro-physical structure of that system. This is so commonsense that it is usually taken for granted but this does not take away from its importance. And to see it, all you need to do is just look around you and see examples of even daily used items that work according to their structures. These systems could be real, such as your car, or virtual. As an example of the latter, consider, the following equation:

$$f(x) = 2x$$

In mathematics, this equation is called a "function" (and thus shown with the letter "f") which operates on the input "x" to yield the output "2x". The English interpretation of this equation is that for any value you plug into x, the function multiplies it by two. If you input 2, the function outputs 4, if you input 10, it outputs 20, and so on. If this sounds familiar, it should. This function is one of the many others that are electronically built into your pocket calculator, smart phone, and desktop computer, as well as into thousands of other types of electronic machines. Regardless of where you find it, the outcome of the mathematical operation of this function is the direct result of its virtual structure. It is perfectly obvious also that one would not get the same results if any of the structural components of this equation were to be changed (like replacing the "2" with a "3").

As for non-virtual SFR examples, there are plenty of them around you too. Your mechanical wrist watch (if you still wear one these days) functions exactly according to its physical structure. Any even minor damage, say to one of its cogwheels, would either stop it completely or would result in its malfunction that would take you to your appointment at a wrong time.

Advancing into the domain of the "Living", and starting from the SFR in microstructures, we could look at that of DNA (shown in Figure 5 of Chapter 7). The very function of the DNA, as a hereditary information molecule and at least through the present evolutionarily established mechanisms, depends on its double-helical structure which, in turn, is a consequence of its primary build (the base-sugar-phosphate sequence shown in Figure 2 of Chapter 7). For instance, Danish scientists in 1991 made polymeric (or *multi*-molecular) compounds in which individual nucleic bases of DNA (those A, T, C, G, and U units which are present in DNA and RNA and were describes in Chapter 7) were attached as side chains of a derivative of glycine, one of the 20 natural amino acids. This was an attempt to prepare, and study the properties and applications of, DNA and RNA mimics which they called *"peptide nucleic acids, PNAs"* (2). Although PNAs had the ability to stably bind to normal DNA and RNA analogues, they had poor water solubility, which was an important shortcoming for applications in biological processes. Furthermore, PNAs could not be recognized by the enzymes involved in the DNA replication, transcription, and translation mechanisms (Chapter 7). Although PNAs have found important uses in molecular biology, they turned out not to be useful as hereditary and reproductive agents such as genes.

Taking one step higher on the "taxonomic ladder", the relationship between structure and function could readily be appreciated in the *Plantae* kingdom as well. The area is too large to be covered all in one chapter so let's suffice by citing just one example: I am sure most of you have noticed the way plants like grape vines, zucchinis, and cucumbers, that do not have a strong enough body to stand on their own, attach themselves to neighboring plants or other stronger bodies for support. They do this by growing these thread-like extensions called tendrils that extend out of branches and as soon as they sense (by coming into contact with) an external object, they twist around it. The next, and more amazing step, is that the tendrils then curl around themselves to shorten their length, and as a result, pull the rest of the plant both up and closer to the supporting body. And pulling the plant up creates a tensional force due to the weight of the plant. Now catch this: The stronger the tensional force, the more the tendrils twist, and therefore, the shorter they become. And the shorter they become the higher the plant is pulled.

But wait a second! Even with all that, how do they manage to do this while both ends of their tendrils are tied up (one to the body of the plant and the other to that of the supporting object)? Here comes another "when-there-is-a-will-there-is-a-way" case, masterfully demonstrated by Mother Nature. It turns out that the tendril divides itself into two separate segments each twisting in an opposite direction with respect to the other. That way, neither the plant itself nor the supporting body has to turn and twist with the tendril. And how the same string, with its ends tied up, could not only twist around itself, but twist around itself in opposite directions? Easy when solved: By creating a "buffer zone" in between the two oppositely twisting segments. The segments are separated by a short and straight (non-twisting) length which had been known to scientists for some time. What was not known was *how* the plants do this. This last question was answered by scientists at Harvard. In an elegant piece of work, Gerbode, *et al.* showed that inside of each delicate tendril there is a ribbon whose cells on one side are stiffened and shortened compared to the cells on the other side, and thus causing the twisting towards the stiffened side (3, 4). To prove this, the investigators made model ribbons from a stiff fabric and copper wire, connected sideways, that could mimic the movements of cucumber plant tendrils. This model could demonstrate that the tendrils "functioned" in the way that they did as a result of the mechanical difference in the structural features of their cells, that is, the cells on one side were stiffer and less flexible than those on the other. And this structural difference, of course, was the result of differences in the types and arrangements of atoms and molecules that made those cells.

We may need not much effort, therefore, to realize that the principle of SFR is universal, and thus, could be extrapolated to the *Animalia* kingdom as well. And that's what we do in the next chapter.

Notes

[1] One might recall the history behind the decoding of DNA structure, Francis Crick and James Watson, and Linus Pauling, when Pauling was denied a passport to visit with Rosalind Franklin in England and evaluate her X-ray crystallography data on DNA. Should he have been able to make that trip, there could have been a good chance that he published the DNA structure before Crick and Watson and become *the* only scientist with a whopping *"Three-Time Nobel Laureate"* title. See http://scarc.library.oregonstate.edu/coll/pauling/dna/narrative/page12.html

REFERENCES

1. Hansch C and Leo A, *Exploring QSAR*, American Chemical Society, Washington, D.C., 1995.
2. Nielsen PE, Egholm M, Berg RH, Buchardt O, Sequence-Selective Recognition of DNA by Strand Displacement with a Thymine-Substituted Polyamide, Science, 254 (5037): 1497–500, 1991. DOI: 10.1126/science.1962210. PMID 1962210
3. Gerbode SJ, Puzey JR, McCormick, AG, Mahadevan, L, How the Cucumber Tendril Coils and Overwinds, *Science*, 337: 1087-1091, 2012.
4. Also see http://www.theguardian.com/science/2012/aug/30/secrets-climbing-plants-tendrils

CHAPTER 9

Genes, Brains, and Behavior

EVEN IF WE DID NOT know this already (which I doubt), after reading the information given in Chapter 7, we should have no problem appreciating the importance of genes due to their two major functions: 1. Replicating (copying) organisms to produce their offspring, and 2. Determining the structural features, and thus traits, of genetically replicated organisms. And from the information discussed in Chapter 8, we now should know that "structural features" directly determine the specific characteristic of an organism. These functions not only include the *physical* (*e.g.*, overall shape and size, color, *etc.*) and *physiological* (*e.g.*, hot-blooded or cold-blooded, gill-breathing or lung-breathing, *etc.*) features of the organism but the *behavioral* traits, particularly in more advanced organisms. In this context, "behavioral" refers to a very wide range of psychological traits such as reacting to the environmental effectors, stimuli, and variables, as well as decision making, or a combination of all of these. Those traits in combination with physical and physiological characteristics lead to what is collectively known as *"temperament"*. Temperament by definition includes all personality traits of an individual (*1*). The old school of philosophy, as old as Hippocrates (*ca.* 460-370 BCE), recognized four different temperaments for any given individual and in an individual, the proportional combination of these four temperaments determined what type of a person that individual could possibly be. Those four temperaments were called sanguine, choleric, melancholic, and phlegmatic. The great Iranian physician and polymath, Avicenna (or Abu Ali Seena, 980-1037) even included mental capacity, emotions, moral character, self-awareness, movements, and dreams in the classification of temperamental traits in his *Canon of Medicine* (published in 1025) which was a standard text in many major medical schools around the world (2). According to the old-school theory, temperaments resulted from the effects of The Four Humors. The word *"humor"*, not to be confused with the one meaning "comic", is a translation of the Greek word *"chymos"* which means juice or sap. It was believed that people's characters and personalities (temperaments), with all consequences thereof, are results of the existence and actions of these four humors in their bodies. The old-school's four humors and their associated temperaments are shown in the table below.

Humor	Producing Organ	Temperament	Character
Phlegm	Brain/lung	Phlegmatic	Calm, patient
Blood	Liver	Sanguine	Cheerful, positive
Yellow bile	Spleen	Choleric	Excitable, ambitious
Black bile	Gallbladder	Melancholic	Quiet, analytical, serious

It was also believed that the overall character of an individual would depend on the overall proportions of these four humors in the body. The higher the production of one humor, the more predominant *its* corresponding temperament will be in the individual's character. The four humors were also believed to be responsible for the level of healthiness of humans. Thus, a complete balance (but not necessarily equality) of humors meant a perfectly healthy person.

With the increasing advances made in physical sciences in general and neuroscience in particular, the belief in, and the importance of, the Theory of Four Humors has become more and more obsolete (and mostly so, since the later years of the nineteenth century). Today, it is a scientifically well-supported fact that personality and temperaments are primarily the direct results of the brains structure and even of the whole central nervous system, although the general bodily conditions (structure, and physiology) could also play some secondary roles. A wealth of information is available in the reported literature on brain-behavior and brain-temperament-personality relationship research, but looking at some representative examples in this chapter may clear the point of our discussion a bit further. Before doing that, however, let's take a quick look at the "action center" of the human psyche, a.k.a., *The Brain*.[1]

The human brain (or cerebrum as its major outer part is called) is composed of fatty tissue and is located inside of the skull. It weighs about 1.3-1.5 kg (or about 2% of the total mass of the body) with a volume of 1135 Cm^3 in women and 1260 Cm^3 in men. The organ consists of neurons (or nerve cells), glial cells (or neuron-supporting cells), and blood vessels. There are about 90 billion neurons and an almost equal number of non-neuron cells in an adult human brain. The outer surface of the brain is called the cerebral cortex which is divided into two hemispheres (cortices) along the body's sagittal plane (3). The hemispheres are divided by MLF (medial longitudinal fissure) but are also connected by *corpus callosum*, a flat bridge made of neural fibers. The cerebral cortex processes memory, cognition, thoughts, perception, attention, language, consciousness, and awareness. Cerebral cortex in humans is about 2-4 mm thick and is wrinkled to form ridges (or gyri) and furrows (or sulci) (4). This wrinkling produces a rather large surface area which makes it possible for the brain to accommodate as large a number of neurons as possible. You may think of the wrinkles as another structural trick played by Nature, in response to the very limited (and very rigid) availability of the intracranial space. This was crucial when more and more intelligence, and therefore more neurons, was needed for humans' survival and for improving their quality of life. In both hemispheres, the cerebral cortex is divided into four lobes called frontal, parietal, temporal, and occipital lobes. Within each lobe there are specialized cortical areas for different functional roles such as motor control and language. As is common in all vertebrae, human brain consists of three segments known as forebrain, midbrain, and hindbrain. And as a typical mammalian brain, human brain has special features such as a six-layered cerebral cortex and a number of associated structures like the hippocampi and amygdala. The six-layered part of the cortex is called neocortex which is the largest part of the cerebral cortex and controls imagination, sensory perception, spatial reasoning, conscious and abstract thoughts, motor commands, and language. The rest of the cerebral cortex is called allocortex with three to four layers of neurons.

Hippocampus (or hippocampi in plural form because there are two of them, one in each half of the brain) is a structure very much looking like seahorses (Greek: *hippos*, "horse" and *kampos*, "sea monster") located under the cerebral cortex, deep in the medial temporal lobes of the human brain (5). Hippocampus has important functions in processing and consolidating information from short-term memory to long-term memory, and also in spatial navigation. The latter function provides the ability to process information about one's environment, locational position, and making decisions about moving around, finding one's way, *etc*. In Alzheimer's patients, hippocampus is one of the early-hit areas of the brain to cause dementia and disorientation.

Amygdala are a couple of densely neuron-packed and almond-shaped structures (Greek: *amygdale*, "almond") located deep inside of the temporal lobes and play primary roles in processing information and memory, decision-making, and emotional reactions (6).

Moving down and towards the back of the brain, we find the brainstem, a segment that connects the cerebrum to the spinal cord and itself is composed of three segments, midbrain, pons, and *medulla oblongata*. The brainstem provides sensory and motor innervation for the face and neck through the cranial nerves and connects the brain with the peripheral nervous system. It also plays major roles in the regulation of the cardiac and respiratory functions (heart rate, blood pressure, breathing), swallowing, consciousness, and sleep-wake cycles.

Some of the other important parts of the brain are:

The cerebellum (Latin: little brain) is located in the back and at the bottom of the brain and almost at the top of the brainstem (7). It is a compact structure as it contains about half of the brain neurons. Cerebellum receives signals from peripheral nerves through the spinal cord and from different parts of the brain and integrates the signals to produce balanced and fine-tuned voluntary movements.

Thalamus is located between cerebral cortex and midbrain. It regulates sleep, consciousness, and alertness, as well as relaying sensory and motor signals to the cerebral cortex.

Hypothalamus, located under thalamus (Greek: *hypo*, "under"), is a collection of small nuclei with different functions. One of the functions of hypothalamus is connecting the nervous system to the endocrine system via the pituitary gland. The pituitary gland is part of the hypothalamus itself. For those who have never heard of it, the endocrine system is a collection of glands whose secretions directly enters the circulation system (the blood) to be carried to the target organs. These glands include the pineal and pituitary glands of the brain, as well as the thyroid, parathyroid and adrenal glands, pancreas, ovaries in women, and testes in men.

Optic tectum (superior colliculus) is located in the mid brain. Among some other functions, it receives visual stimuli from retina that leads to vision (8).

Basal ganglia are located at the base of the forebrain. A network of nuclei, it is interconnected to cerebral cortex, thalamus, and the brainstem, and controls learning (involving thoughts, experience, and senses), development and control of habits, eye movements, and emotions (9).

Olfactory bulb is a structure contained in the forebrain which is involved with olfaction or the sense of smell.

So, the discovery of these control and processing centers in our brains, and the existence of the connection of each of them to one or more of our mechanical, physiological, and psychological functions clearly point to a taken-for-granted and rarely noticed conclusion: *Brains are us.* Who we are, what we do, and how we manage our lives and react to the environment we live in and to people we deal with, decisions that we make, *etc.*, are all products of this soft and wrinkled mass we have inside of our heads. It is the *physical* nature of this organ that determines our temperaments, behavior, and actions at any given moment during our lifetime. And if we take into account the interplays and interactions among the brains (or its equals) of all creatures whatever, then it should be easy to recognize for this organ a major role in a major portion of what has been going on in this world (a "major portion" because there are other determining factors coming into play too as we shall see later in this book).

Furthermore, let's not forget that the exact structure of the brain, on which temperaments and other individual-specific characters such as psychology, physiology, physique, and whatever else that make an individual who he is, is dictated by the genes of that individual. How so? Remember the material covered in Chapter 7 about the genetic code and gene expression? Every single molecule in the make-up of the brains, its neuronal connections, and the way that every particle of it come together to form its three-dimensional structure, is the manifestation of our inherited genetic code. We inherit the genetic information package from our ancestors and our parents, and whatever we become depends, to a significant extent, on the order in which those four letters of the genetic language, G, A, C, and T (chapter 7), are strung together in our chromosomes. The relationship between genes and brains structure, and therefore, between genes and who we are, has been (and is being) studied quite extensively, and in major part, through brain mapping experiments. These experiments have shown not only the existence of such relationships but also the correlation of the results with those of behavioral studies (*10*). As mentioned above, one of the functions of the cerebral cortex is cognition. Many gene-brain structure studies have shown that a measure of cognitive ability, known as the *"g"factor*, is highly heritable.

In experiments using 3-dimentional brain mapping techniques, it has been shown that there was increasing brain structure similarities in subjects with increasing genetic similarities (*11*). In the same study, researchers reported that genetic factors significantly affected language areas of the frontal cortex which is linked to the "g" factor or the measure of cognition ability.

In yet another study on 1,583 14-year-old students, researchers showed that an altered version of a gene named *NPTN*, resulted in a thinner-than-normal grey matter in the left brain of some of the students which, in turn, resulted in a weaker performance in intellectual abilities evaluation tests compared to subjects with normal copies of the gene *(12)*. Grey matter is the part of the brains and central nervous system that is made of neurons whose axons (or neural cell stems) lack a fatty insulating substance called myelin. The *NPTN* gene encodes a protein called neuroplastin (NPTN) that affects the neuronal synapses (points of connection between two neurons) in the central nervous system which facilitates neuron-to-neuron communications. A mutation in this gene apparently alters the NPTN protein and compromises the cellular communications, which in turn, results in weaker intellectual abilities.[2]

An interesting aspect of the genes-brains-behavior, which has been the subject of much active research, is the effect of specific genes on the structure of the brains, which in turn, leads to a predisposition of the affected individual to antisocial and psychopathic behaviors. This hypothesis is coined *"Genes to Brain to Antisocial Behavior"* model in a review article by Adrian Raine with the same title *(13)*. As an example, Raine cites a common polymorphism (various forms of the same gene) in the *MAOA* gene which codes for the enzyme monoamine oxidase A (MAOA, a protein). There is a technique in molecular genetics called *"knocking"* where a gene may be neutralized (or knocked out) or reactivated (or knocked in) that is routinely used when the exact role(s) of a particular gene in a given organism is to be determined. It has been shown that when the *MAOA* gene is knocked out in mice, the animals turn into aggressive and fighting creatures. Mouse is an animal model regularly used in medical, biological, and pharmaceutical research that happens to be a mammal like us (no offense). Interestingly, when the gene is knocked back in, the mice once again become normal, gentle, and "civilized" rodents *(14)*. Statistics-backed reproducible studies on humans have also confirmed the role of *MAOA* gene in antisocial behavior *(15, 16)*.

A question that we may now ask is, in addition to the gene knock-out experimental data, what other evidences do we have that proves the relationship between the *MAOA* gene and antisocial behavior? To answer this question, we must first know what neurotransmitters are. Neurotransmitters (also called chemical messengers) are molecules that transmit signals from neurons (or nerve cells) to a target cell such as another neuron or a muscle cell. A chemical called "serotonin" is such a molecule, a neurotransmitter. The enzyme (reminder: enzymes are some kind of protein) that the *MAOA* gene codes for, which is called monoamine oxidase A or MAOA, breaks down (or digests) serotonin. It has been shown that the amount of serotonin in subjects with antisocial behavior is lower than that in normal subjects. Therefore, it was concluded that a particular polymorphism of this gene overexpresses the enzyme MAOA which leads to an over-breakdown of serotonin, thus resulting in lowered levels of this neurotransmitter in the blood, which in turn, results in antisocial behavior. Furthermore, it has also been shown that in male subjects with a common polymorphism of the *MAOA* gene, the volume of amygdala, and some other brain structures that are involved in emotions control, is reduced by about 8% (*17*). This compromise in the size of amygdala leads to antisocial behavior in the affected individuals.

Another very interesting study which has been recently reported, is the relationship between human genes and happiness. A research group at the Vrije Universiteit Amsterdam in the Netherlands, has shown that there is a relationship between people's genetic make-up and how happy (or sad) they feel and in general between genes and quality of life. While initially these researchers had found that there were only two locations on human genome that contain mood-controlling genes, the number grew to about twenty locations later on. The study was done on around 300,000 people and the results reproducibly confirmed the "gene-quality of life" relationship (*18*, *19*).

With all its significance, our inherited genetic blueprint is not *the* only determining factor in making us who we are and how we make our moves and decisions in life, and therefore, this may be the time we get familiarized with the term *"Epigenetics"*. Epigenetics is a relatively new branch of genetics sciences which studies the environmental effects on cellular gene expression (20). These environmental effects may, in turn, change the structure of some of the gene expression products, such as the brain and central nervous system, the related enzymes and neurotransmitters, and thereby, temperaments and behavior.

Perhaps one of the more common epigenetic factors is mother's stress during pregnancy. As was mentioned before, mouse is a very good experimental model for early-stage medical and scientific studies where the results might be later applied to human clinical studies. It has also been shown that rodents react to stress in very much the same way as humans do. When pregnant female mice were put under stress early into their pregnancy (days 1-7), their male offspring showed a 10% reduction in their body size, reduced cognitive abilities, and increased sensitivity to stress, all results of a modified brain structure due to induction of stress into their gestation environment (21, 22).

In another interesting piece of work, researchers studied the effects of maternal vaginal microbiota on the brain development of the offspring. The term *"microbiota"* refers to the collection of microorganisms that colonize, and benefit from, a niche in the body (such as the gut, skin, or sexual organs). They do this in either a commensal (organisms benefit but cause no harm to host), a symbiotic (both organism and host benefit), or a pathogenic (organism induces harm to host) manner. During pregnancy, exposure of the neonate to mother's vaginal microbiota leads to the development of baby's gut microbiota, providing the primary source for their immune system maturation and metabolism. The process happens during a critical time window of the nervous system development which may also imply that during the early life, there may be a *"crosstalk"* between the neonate's gut and brains. So, any disturbance to the prenatal vaginal microbiota (such as stress to mother) could be a factor in the formation of long-term neurodevelopmental diseases as well as deficiencies in brain development with the end result of perturbed temperament, personality, and behavior developments. To prove this correlation, these workers showed that maternal stress in pregnant mice altered some proteins related to vaginal immunity and to the abundance of *Lactobacilli*, one of the major vaginal microorganisms. The lowered levels of *Lactobacillus* led to an imbalance of the gut microbiota of the offspring, which in turn, disturbed the balance of amino acid profile in the developing brain (23).

When we talk about the environmental effects on the brains, we should also include environments a bit farther than mother's body (the so-called extrauterine *vs.* intrauterine phenomena). In fact, there may be more coming to our brains from the outside world than our moms' body. These include social, chemical, and physical factors to name a few. Chemicals known as neurotoxins, for instance, affect the normal metabolism of the central nervous system to cause some abnormality in the brain's structure which in turn would lead to some kind of psychiatric disorder. Let's look at one of the oldest of neurotoxins known to man, the soft, heavy, and grey metal, lead. Lead poisoning has been known since the ancient times with a famous case being that of some of the Roman emperors, including Nero, to a point that some even connect lead poisoning to the fall of the Roman Empire (24). Lead poisoning occurs when traces of the metal enter the body through ingestion, breathing, or skin absorption. Upon ingestion, the metal substitutes itself for some metabolically needed metals. This could, in turn, lead to the development of a number of serious maladies. One of the effects is the impairment in the development of the brain and other parts of the central nervous system (CNS). In the still-developing CNS of children, lead poisoning results in a reduction in the overall number of neurons and the overall brain volume, which leads to learning and cognition impairments (25). Eventually, these deficiencies would have some adverse effects on the personality and temperament of the poisoned individual.

It should be noted that the environmental effects on the brain do not necessarily need to be negative. Good climate, clean air, good nutrition, low-level or non-existent stress (both maternal and neonatal), *etc.*, all may contribute to a positive development of the brain and CNS of a newborn. The message here is that personalities, temperaments, extent of mental sharpness, and all other characteristics that further lead to the *general behavior of* an individual, all depend primarily on the physical structure of the brain and the CNS which themselves are the products of genetics as well as of the environment, a concept known as *"nature versus nurture"*, although in my opinion, *all* is naturally, *Nature*. We shall see how in the remaining chapters.

NOTES

[1] The word "psyche" (Latin: *psūchê*) is a Septuagint translation of the Hebrew word *"nephesh"* which itself entered Judaism after the Babylonian Exile and as a result of the Persian (ancient Iranian) philosophy influence on the post-exile Jewish culture. Although in versions of the Bible it has been translated as "soul" (an immortal entity independent from the physical body), nephesh really means "living being" itself without implementing anything supernatural.

[2] By convention, genes have the same name as the proteins they encode. Genes' names are shown in italicized letters whereas those of their proteins are not.

REFERENCES

1. Clark LA, Watson D, Mineka S, Temperament, Personality, and the Mood and Anxiety Disorders, *J Ab Psych*, 103 (1): 103-116, 1994.
2. Lutz PL, *The Rise of Experimental Biology: An Illustrated History*, Humana Press, 2002, p. 60, ISBN 0896038351.
3. Pelvig DP, Pakkenberg H, Stark AK, Pakkenberg B, Neocortical Glial Cell Numbers in Human Brains, *Neurobiol Agi*, 29 (11): 1754–1762, 2008.
4. Kandel ER, Schwartz JH, Jessell TM, *Principles of Neural Science (4th Ed.)*, McGraw-Hill, USA, 2000, ISBN 0-8385-7701-6.
5. Amaral D, and Lavenex P, In Anderson P, Morris R, Amaral D, Bliss T, O'Keefe J, *The Hippocampus Book* (1st Ed.), p. 37, Oxford University Press, New York, ISBN 978-0-19-510027-3.
6. Moga MM, *et al.*, Organization of Cortical, Basal Forebrain and Hypothalamic Afferents to the Parabrachial Nucleus in the Rat, *J Comp Neu*, 295 (4): 624-661, 1990. DOI: 10.1002/cne.902950408
7. Timmann D and Daum I, Cerebellar contributions to cognitive functions: A progress report after two decades of research, In: *Cerebellum*, Springer, New York, 2007. DOI: 10.1080/14734220701496448
8. Benevento LA and Gregg PS, The Organization of Projections of the Retinorecipient and Nonretinorecipient Nuclei of the Pretectal Complex and Layers of the Superior Colliculus to the Lateral Pulvinar and Medial Pulvinar in the Macaque Monkey, *Sci Dir*, 1983.
9. Stocco A, Lebiere C, Anderson JR, Conditional Routing of Information to the Cortex: A Model of the Basal Ganglia's Role in Cognitive Coordination, *Psych Rev*, 117 (2): 541–74, 2010. DOI: 10.1037/a0019077

10. Toga AW and Thompson PM, Genetics of Brain Structure and Intelligence, *Ann Rev Neurosci*, 28: 1-23, 2005. DOI: 10.1146/annurev.neuro.28.061604.135655
11. Thompson PM, Genetic Influences on Brain Structure, *Nature Neurosci*, 4: 1253 – 1258, 2001. DOI: 10.1038/nn758
12. Desrivieres S, *et al.*, Single Nucleotide Polymorphism in the Neuroplastin Locus Associates with Cortical Thickness and Intellectual Ability in Adolescentset, *Mol Psy*, 20 (2): 263-74, 2015. DOI: 10.1083/mp.2013.197
13. Raine, A, From Genes to Brain to Antisocial Behavior, *Curr Dir Psychol Sci*, 17 (5): 323-327, 2008. DOI: 1467-8721.2008.00599
14. Cases O, *et al.*, Aggressive Behavior and Altered Amounts of Brain Serotonin and Norepinephrine in Mice Lacking MAOA, *Science*, 268 (5218): 1763-1766, 1995. DOI: 10.1126/science.7792602
15. Caspi A, *et al.*, Role of Genotype in the Cycle of Violence in Maltreated Children, *Science*, 297: 851-854, 2002. DOI: 10.1126/science.1072290
16. Kim-Cohen L, *et al.*, *MAOA*, Maltreatment, and Gene–Environment Interaction Predicting Children's Mental Health: New Evidence and a Meta-Analysis, *Mol Psychiatry*, 11: 903–913, 2006. DOI: 10.1038/sj.mp.4001851
17. Meyer-Lindenberg A, *et al.*, Neural Mechanisms of Genetic Risk for Impulsivity and Violence in Humans, *Proc Nat Acad Sci, USA*, 103: 6269-6274, 2006. DOI: 10.1073/pnas.0511311103
18. Sprangers MA, *et al.*, Biological Pathways, Candidate Genes, and Molecular Markers Associated with Quality-of-Life Domains: An Update, *Qual Life Res*, 23 (7): 1997-2013, 2014. DOI: 10.1007/s11136-014-0656-1
19. Sprangers MA, *et al.*, Which Patient will Feel Down, Which Will Be Happy? The Need to Study the Genetic Disposition of

Emotional States, *Qual Life Res*, 19 (10): 1429-1437, 2010. DOI: 10.1007/s11136-010-9652-2

20. Francis RC, *Epigenetics: How Environment Shapes Our Genes*, W. W Norton, New York, 2011.

21. Mueller BR and Bale TL, Early Prenatal Impact on Coping Strategies and Learning is Sex Dependent, *Physiol Behav*, 2007, 91 (1): 55-65, 2007. DOI: 10.1016/j.physbeh.2007.01.017

22. Mueller BR and Bale TL, Sex-Specific Programming of Offspring Emotionality After Stress Early in Pregnancy, *J Neurosci*, 28 (36):9055-9065, 2008. DOI: https://doi.org/10.1523/JNEUROSCI.1424-08.2008

23. Jasarevic E, et al., Alterations in the Vaginal Microbiome by Maternal Stress are Associated with Metabolic Reprogramming of the Offspring Gut and Brain, *Endocrinology*, 156 (9): 3265-3276, 2015. DOI: http://dx.doi.org/10.1210/en.2015-1177

24. Nriagu JO, Saturnine Gout among Roman Aristocrats. Did Lead Poisoning Contribute to the Fall of the Empire? *N Eng J Med*, 308 (11): 660-663, 1983. DOI: 10.1056/NEJM198303173081123

25. Bellinger DC, Lead, *Pediatrics*, 113 (4) (Suppl. 3), 1016-1022, 2004. DOI: pediatrics.aappublications.org/content/113/Supplement_3/1016

CHAPTER 10

Are We All Set?

―⚊―

IN THE LAST EIGHT CHAPTERS we hopefully got familiarized with *The Beginning* according to the Big Bang theory as well as some of its products and consequences: Atoms, molecules, their coming together, what happens when they come together, what type of assemblies they may form, how the structures of these ensembles may affect what they do (the structure-activity relationship), how genes and genetics are, in fact, phenomena that have their roots in molecular structure and function, how genes may affect brains formation, and how the brain structure may be related to our *"Selves"*, how we behave, make decisions, and react to our environments. If you detect a pattern here, congratulations, you're on the right track. And if you don't, you may still be on the right track because you're reading this book (!) and because in the rest of this book, I shall share with you a few more pieces of information which would hopefully illuminate for you not only the *"pattern"* I just mentioned, but would also guide you to the *"path"* to the intended message of this book, and finally to *"The Message"* itself. To do that though, we would need to again change gears: From strictly physical scientific topics we have been covering so far to the realm of Philosophy. We would need to do this gear-shifting because philosophy and science shall ultimately merge at the end of this writing to guide us to our intended conclusion.

The part of philosophy which we need to touch on here is reflected in the ancient word, or better said, the school of thought, *"Determinism"* (*1, 2*). But before I talk about that subject, let me explain a related term, *"Causality"* (*3*). In philosophy, Causality is the *relationship* between an event or a process (referred to as the *"Cause"*) and the consequential event or process (the *"Effect"*). Causality may propagate *indefinitely* by the Effect so that the Effect itself becomes the Cause for the next Effect, and so on. Any given event or process may have a multitude of causes, referred to as *"Causal Factors"*. For any given event or process (at the time of its occurrence), all of its Causal Factors lie in its past while all of its Effects lie in its future.

Note: For the sake of clarity and simplicity, I shall use the word *"Event"* to semantically include (and replace) words such as "process", "decision", "action", "reaction", *etc.*, in the rest of this writing.

Now going back to Determinism, a philosophical belief most of us may be familiar with already, albeit without necessarily knowing what it was called. There is more than one way to define Determinism but all of them basically propose that any and every given Event in the universe is determined, out of necessity and through the process of Causality, by a certain Cause (or certain Causes) which has (or have) acted sometime in that Event's past. The resulting Event may itself become the Cause for other Events which lie in its future.

Naturally, one of the immediate intellectual reactions to this proposition would be asking this question: "If everything is determined, what about our Freewill?" Freewill, huh? "Yep, of course!", you may say, "isn't it supposed to be the greatest gift we humans have been endowed with?" "Isn't it *The Right* that all of us have been born with and shall die with? Am I, the mighty *Homo sapiens*, not supposed to do as I please in and with my life? Did I not just buy the car I liked, eat the meal I wanted to eat, and marry the one I was in love with? Can't you people see I do as I wish, whenever I want, wherever I want? Of course, I have my own Freewill!" .... Well, let's see. Let's get out of the euphoria of our belief in human Freewill for a while and go back into the cold, indiscriminate, but realistic and honest universe of science in search of an answer. After all, it may be in there, in the realm of science, and there only, that the virtual barriers to our true visions about Life may crumble and fall, and we will be finally able to see the truth, regardless of its color and taste. But first, some definitions:

From the point of view of Freewill (4), there are two interpretations of Determinism:

1. **Incompatibilism:** As the name implies, Incompatibilism suggests that Determinism and Freewill are incompatible, and therefore, are mutually exclusive. As such, if Determinism is true and Freewill is an illusion, we have *Hard Determinism*. And if Freewill is true and Determinism is false, we will be talking about *Libertarianism*.
2. **Compatibilism:** Compatibilism, on the other hand, accepts the co-existence of Determinism and Freewill. It holds, however, that Freewill is *not* the ability to make decisions or choices independently of prior causes but is the freedom of *not* making a decision or a choice (5). This kind of determinism is called *Soft Determinism*.

The doctrine of Determinism has been on the to-do list of many scientists and philosophers including the world-famous Iranian mathematician, poet, and philosopher, Hakim Omar Khayyam (1048-1141), as well as Baruch Spinoza (1632-1677), Gottfried Leibniz (1646-1716), and some more modern figures, from Ralph Waldo Emerson (1803-1882), Albert Einstein, and Niels Bohr (1885-1962), to the contemporary physicist and cosmologist, Stephen Hawking, and philosopher Ted

Honderich (1933). It should be emphasized, however, that there may be some variations in the interpretation of Determinism as believed by each of these and other proponents of this doctrine. Historically, the beginnings of the idea of Determinism go back to the ancient era and to the atomist philosophers, Leucippus (5th century BCE) and Democritus (*ca.* 460 – 370 BCE).

Determinism or Determinism-related philosophies have long existed in both Eastern and non-Eastern cultures. In the Indian philosophies, and only as limited to its provocation of the cause-and-effect principle, perhaps "Karma" is a concept that may be considered close to Determinism. Putting it in simple words, this school believes that good deeds, thoughts, and words beget good effects and bad ones beget bad effects. Causality, therefore, plays a central role and can be considered a similarity between Karma and Determinism (6).

The ancient Greek philosophers were divided over Determinism. Atomists such as Leucippus and Democritus were perhaps the earliest in expressing their approval for Determinism. A quote ascribed to Leucippus goes *"Nothing happens at random, but everything from rational principle and of necessity."*

Epicurus (341-270 BCE) while an atomist too, did not believe in Determinism in the same way as Leucippus and Democritus did. He believed that while all matter is made of indivisible particles (or atoms), their "swervy" (author-made derivative of the verb "to swerve") behavior would make the ultimate outcome of their activities unpredictable, and thus, undetermined. It is believed that because of this he might have been leaning towards Freewill.

In the Enlightenment-Era Europe, the development of newly discovered rules of physics reinforced the cause-and-effect concept. An example of these was the findings of Isaac Newton (1643-1727). Newton's first law of motion (described in Chapter 11) states that in an inertial frame of reference (simply stated, an inertial frame of reference is a portion of space in which measurements are taken), an object either remains at rest or moves at a constant velocity unless acted upon by an external force. Looking at it from a philosophical point-of-view, the law means nothing other than the phenomenon of cause-and-effect. Therefore, some scientists interpreted it to validate the Determinism proposition. It might have also influenced the views of the French mathematician and philosopher, René Descartes (1596-1650) when he proposed that living things, just as the non-living matter, obeyed the laws of physics, and therefore, the material part of the world was strictly deterministic. Descartes, however, did believe in the Freewill of the human soul, which according to his ideas, was immaterial.

Another French scientist, Pierre-Simon Laplace (1749-1827), was so firm a believer in both the Newtonian Laws and Determinism that he suggested that a super intelligence which has an accurate knowledge of the forces and positions of *all* particles in the Universe, and which is also equipped with means of accurately analyzing that knowledge, would have in its possession a formula capable of predicting the whole of the future as clearly as it could see the past. This hypothetical proposition is known as *"Laplace's Demon"* (7).

In the modern era (the 20th and the current centuries) at least a percentage of the scientific opinion on Determinism and Freewill has been significantly affected, and sometimes even influenced, by Quantum and Chaos theories. To some, both of these theories may imply, and be the proof of, a *perception* of uncertainty, randomness, and unpredictability of the Universe. In case you are not familiar with Quantum and Chaos theories already, I shall tell you what they are in the next two chapters, as well as offering a Determinism-related alternative view about them.

Whatever the origins, the current Determinism doctrine falls into more than one kind, mostly with very close (and sometimes confusing) definitions. Let's sample a few:

Causal Determinism: The definitions of Causal Determinism is very similar to the general definition given above for Determinism (*8*). To avoid confusion, and in order to remember them in a more organized fashion, it may be a good idea to itemize the outstanding aspects of each class (remember these when reading Chapter 13 too). The Causal Determinism doctrine proposes that:

1. All Events are necessarily caused by antecedent Events and the ambient conditions present at the time of the causation.
2. The causation process leading to an Event is affected by, and is a function of, laws of Nature.
3. The causation process is a continuum without any interruption.
4. No effect in the Universe is without a cause and neither is it self-caused.

There are two subclasses of Causal Determinism known as *"Nomological Determinism"* and *"Necessitarianism"*. When looked at closely, their definitions are fundamentally the same as that of the Causal Determinism with the former indicating that past and present dictate the future as necessitated by solid natural laws, and the latter suggesting that there is only one way, and one way only, for the world to be.

Predeterminism: The name says it all: Events are *pre*-determined and are set in advance as how to take shape in their future. Here too, it is believed that the world consists of an unbroken chain of events which goes back to the very beginning of the Universe. Each Event is caused by an earlier one under the direct and strict control of the natural laws, but all events are determined from the beginning. As such, a hypothetical observer could have known what would happen in the future, *had* the observer been able to see the "blueprint".

Well, ... don't blame the alert students of this school of thought should they dare ask "if everything is determined according to the Causal Determinism and if everything is determined as per Predeterminsm, what in the world is the difference between the two propositions?" If I were asked this question, I would have answered it by proposing a thought scenario as follows: Let's think of two knitting machines one of which (Machine A) is interfaced with, and operated by, a computer which is equipped with a program for knitting a sweater. The computer program of Machine A has a strictly stepwise feature that guides the knitting parts from one step to the next if and only if the first one is complete, and therefore, each completed step of the process is a cause for starting the next. Furthermore, this process cannot be stopped or interrupted for any length of time. Once the knitting process is started, it would go all the way to the completed sweater. Both machines are fed with threads at the same and sufficient quantities and of exactly the same quality. The other machine (Machine B) lacks the computer but is equipped with special kind of sensors such that, when in contact with the threads, the sensors would automatically send information-encrypted electrical signals to the knitting parts which are then guided to the production of a sweater. The signals are generated strictly *impromptu* and the information encrypted in them is based on the nature of the mutual interactions between the thread and the sensors at each given point in time. And for the sake of the discussion only, let's also assume that both machines could just happen suddenly and spontaneously, that is, they just pop into existence out of nowhere at time zero. Just another one of those *"now-you-don't-see-it-now-you-do"* type of situations (Chapter 2). Also, the very existence of both machines is a cause for their cranking up spontaneously, which in turn, is a cause for knitting through a non-stop and stepwise process all the way to the end of the sweater production.

As I am sure you have figured it out yourself, in this scenario, A was a predeterministic machine while B was a causal-deterministic one. Both machines did the same function of knitting sweaters, with A doing this under the guidance of a *preset* computer program while B had no idea what it would be doing at time zero. Its product sweater (the Event) was produced one step at a time guided by signals that were determined by the *nature* of the sensor-thread interactions (the Cause). It was each Cause, and each Cause only, that determined the nature of each next event.

Fatalism: For those of us who might not have heard of it in this context before, the term "Fatalism" has nothing to do with the adjective word "fatal" meaning "capable of causing death". The philosophical word "Fatalism" is derived from the noun word "fate". Depending what context Fatalism is to be defined in, it may also be subdivided into "Metaphysical Fatalism", "Logical Fatalism", "Theological Fatalism", or simply "Fatalism" if it is defined through Causal Determinism. Fatalism is fundamentally a kind of Determinism which emphasizes on elements of submission, resignation, and basically powerlessness of humans towards their fate (9). It proposes that no matter what we do, we have absolutely no power to change, prevent, or cause the pre-established flow of life's events because "something" (or some "thing") has fixed it for us. As such, Fatalism recognizes the involvement of an omniscient force which has consciously planned, and set into motion, the fate of everybody as well as every *"Thing"*. Accordingly, Fatalism thus recognizes a kind of dualism, that is, the existence of a power outside of the contexture of the physical Universe. This is in contrast with the definition and meaning of Causal Determinism which is based on a universal monism with a physical cause-and-effect operational mechanism. But now what's the difference between Fatalism and Predeterminism? A relevant question as both propositions call for a pre-determined nature of the Universe. The answer is in the dualism and monism aspects of Fatalism and Predeterminism, respectively. The predeterminist believes in the same mechanism as the fatalist except with no intervention from any external forces. According to this view, everything is pre-determined because it's the way the Nature works; Nature came to be on its own and operates on its own terms. Those "terms" are pre-determined naturally and need no outside intervention.

There are several other prefixes with their related definitions for describing different versions of Determinism which I shall not describe here because of two reasons:

1. Although they go through different "channels" of defining the terms, at the end of the day, they would all be describing "Determinism" although some of those channels may not be built on scientific grounds, and
2. Considering the aim of this book and the method employed to realize it, I believe focusing just on Causal Determinism should not only suffice but should also be more compatible with a *scientific* strategy-of-approach. And Science is what has the ultimately legitimate vote. You might have noticed that throughout this book, I have carefully avoided the use of, and resorting to, supernaturalism, superstition, and anything that could not have a solid scientific foundation, justification, and explanation. You may also remember my using the phrase ".. nothing supernatural .." in a few places during the past chapters like, for example, when I was talking about atomic and molecular structures and the mechanism of the genetic system. But there is a difference between the present subject, Determinism, and those of atoms, molecules, and genes. You could easily see the (scientific) evidence for what was discussed about atoms, molecules, and genes in the many

scientific resources which are readily available by clicking a few keys on your computer or other smart devices. That is not exactly the case with some philosophical issues including Determinism. For one thing, philosophy, at least in part, is not a hard science. You can never show people a picture of "Realism" in print or on your computer monitor. Neither could you do a "Pragmatism" litmus test and show by hard evidence that your boss is a "pragmatic" woman. And in the specific case of Determinism, nobody could scan somebody's brains in a PET or MRI machine and say "ok, his brain is showing some deterministic activity right now." And for another, Determinism has been subcategorized into groups for some of which we have no physical and tangible support. Fatalism and Predeterminism, introduced above, are two examples of those subcategories. They belong to a special class which I call the *"just-believe-me (JBM)"* propositions. And JBMs are exactly the types of issues, propositions, and theories that I am trying to avoid in this book. Although the intended take-home message of this book (when one finishes reading it) may not be easily acceptable to some, I have at least tried to present it through, and based on, the available physical-scientific knowledge. After all, among all other conventional types of Determinism, it is the *Physical Determinism*, which in my opinion, is the type that merits a science-based evaluation.

At the same time, the non-JBM interpretations of Determinism may all be considered to be physical science in nature. A research-savvy scientist should be able to propose and design experiments to show correlation(s) between behavioral-, biological-, environmental-, and cultural deterministic events as the *Effects*, and behavioral, biological, environmental, and cultural factors as *Causes*. A very simple example in the biological category is the germination of a plant seed. An active seed is "causally determined" to germinate (the Effect) once in an environment which provides it with water and the right temperature (the Causes), and which also protects it from antagonistic effectors such as extremely high or extremely low heat (light and micronutrients are not initially needed for the germination process to commence). In this book, these conventional and non-JBM subdivisions (the ones mentioned in the last paragraph plus others such as Technological-, Economical-, Linguistic-, *etc.*, Determinism) are all meant to be treated as one type, the *Physical Determinism*, to which I shall refer to as just *Determinism* for simplification.

Okay, so much for definitions and explanation of the differences among these somewhat confusing terms. "Now what?" you may ask, "and what's the relationship between all the information given in the previous chapters to this one?" And I'll answer these questions by first propounding this question: "Now that we are in the twenty-first century, with humanity at the peak of its scientific, technological, and information-gathering achievements (as compared to the other times during its *recorded* past history), how could we analyze, and then prove the validity of , a soft-scientific proposition like Determinism using the available hard-scientific knowledge? Or, in simple words, could we arrive at Determinism through hard science?"

In my opinion, that question could be answered by adopting a two-step approach: In the first step, we need to establish that Determinism is actually capable of being hard-scientifically (or natural-scientifically, since natural sciences are considered hard science) analyzed. In other words, would it be possible *and* meaningful to relate Determinism to natural scientific principles and findings? Having addressed this question, we shall then be able to proceed to the second step and show that Determinism is indeed a scientifically valid proposition.

I shall attempt the taking on of the validation process in the last two chapters of this book (Chapters 13 and 14), but before then, let's look at two more topics not unrelated to the issue of Determinism. These two will be briefly discussed in the following two chapters, Chapter 11 and Chapter 12.

REFERENCES

1. Keil G, Determinism, In: *Encyclopedia of Neuroscience*, pp. 948-952, Springer, 2009. DOI: 10.1007/978-3-540-29678-2_1475
2. van Inwagen P, *An Essay on Free Will*, Oxford University Press, Oxford, 1986, ISBN: 9780198249245.
3. Armstrong DM, *A World of States of Affairs*, pp. 89, 265, Cambridge University Press, Cambridge, ISBN 0-521-58064-1.
4. Caruso GD, *Free Will and Consciousness: A Determinist Account of the Illusion of Free Will*, Lexington Books, 2012, ISBN 0739171364.
5. Campbell J, A Compatibilist Theory of Alternative Possibilities, *Phil Stud*, 88: 319–30, 1997.
6. Bowker J, Karma, In: *The Concise Oxford Dictionary of World Religions*, Oxford University Press, Oxford, 1997.
7. Laplace PS, *A Philosophical Essay on Probabilities*, 6th Edn, Dover Publications, New York, 1951.
8. Hoefer C, Causal Determinism, *The Stanford Encyclopedia of Philosophy* (Spring, 2016 Edition), Edward N. Zalta (Ed.), URL: https://plato.stanford.edu/archives/spr2016/entries/determinism-causal/
9. Rice H, Fatalism, *The Stanford Encyclopedia of Philosophy* (Summer, 2015 Edition), Edward N. Zalta (Ed.), URL: https://plato.stanford.edu/archives/sum2015/entries/fatalism/

CHAPTER 11

Don't Blame the Weatherman: It's a Chaos Out There!

—⚛—

PERHAPS SOME OF THE MOST famous (and useful) laws in science, or in physics specifically, are Newton's Laws of Motion. And they didn't earn their fame and scientific place for nothing as we shall see below. Isaac Newton himself is undoubtedly one of the most brilliant scientists (or "Natural Philosophers" as they were called back in the day) and visionaries of post-Renaissance Europe. His book, *"Philosophiæ Naturalis Principia Mathematica (Mathematical Principles of Natural Philosophy*, or *"Principia"* for short), first published in 1687, is considered one of the important publications in the history of science which started an epoch of revolution in applied physics and engineering. In it, Newton laid a systematic foundation for the classical mechanics by organizing the Laws of Motion as well as the Law of Universal Gravitation, and mathematically derived Kepler's Laws of Planetary motion *(1)*. The latter laws had been experimentally established earlier by another genius, the German mathematician and astronomer Johannes Kepler (1571-1630), and made a significant contribution to Newton's work on gravity. In fact, the significance of Newton's contributions is mostly in his interpretation, generalization, and mathematical organization of observations made by earlier scientists as well as by himself. For instance, his first law of motion (shown below) was a restatement of Galileo Galilei's (1564-1642) ideas and experiments on inertia. A quote from Newton himself recognizes this: *"If I have seen further than others, it is by standing upon the shoulders of giants."* Newton's laws of motion observe three natural principles:

First Law (also known as The Law of Inertia): In an inertial frame of reference, an object continues to stay at rest or keep moving at a constant velocity unless acted upon by an external force.

Second Law: The acceleration (a) imposed on an object by an external force (F), is in the same direction as that of the force, is directly proportional to the net magnitude of the force, and is inversely proportional to the mass (m) of the object such that, $a = F/m$.

Third Law: A force exerted by an object onto a second object (an *Action*) is countered by a force, equal in magnitude but opposite in direction, exerted by the second object onto the first (a *Reaction*).

One of the unique features of these laws was their ability to provide some kind of predictability which was, at the time, either unavailable, unclear, or unknown to an average person of science. The use of these laws, and the related mathematics developed by Newton (also by Gottfried Leibniz) known as *"Calculus"*, made it possible for investigators to be able to predict the velocity or position of an object by using the numerical values for its initial velocity, position, and the forces that acted upon that object. A famous and historical example of the application of these laws was the ability of man to go to, and land on, the Moon and then come back home safely! The Laws make it possible to predict the solar and lunar movements in our solar system, and study and predict paths of comets and other heavenly bodies. In military defense, the Laws could help the design of, for example, *anti*-missile weapons. They may also have the potential of preparing us against unlikely disastrous events such as collision of large comets with our planet. There is evidence that a similar event destroyed dinosaurs and most of the earthly life about 60 million years ago (2, 3). With the laws of motion, we could at least hope that we will send, for example, powerful nuclear bombs to destroy such nasty and uninvited guests in space before they reached our atmosphere.

A point on which I would like to emphasize here, as it relates to the main subject of this book, is that Newton's laws are deterministic in nature, and thus, are based on the Principle of Cause-and-Effect. This is because the Laws allow prediction of the conditions (position, velocity, and force) of an object in a future time once we have information about its initial conditions. As such, the future (of single- and two-body systems) may be seen through the lens of the Newtonian Laws of Motion.

Undoubtedly, these laws produced not only a new wave of excitement (among other positive outcomes), but also provided a powerful means for successfully taking on, and solving, some previously tough and unchallenged problems in physics. I can mentally picture groups of 17th and 18th century scientists bunching together in the pub around the corner to boast about their latest achievements in solving an up-to-then daunting problem in mechanics by using the Laws and the related math.

But like almost everything else in our world, the good days came to an end and the Laws finally met their challenge (albeit not completely as we shall see in Chapter 13). The "Challenge" was called the *"Three-Body Problem"* which had been, in fact, recognized by Newton himself and even discussed in his *Principia*. While scientists could happily use the mathematics of the Laws of Motion and Universal Gravitation to calculate, and therefore predict, the "future" physical conditions of either a single object (or body) or a system composed of two bodies simply by applying the information from their past, it was found that this approach would not work for systems consisting of three or more bodies. This shortcoming has been referred to as the *"Three-Body Problem"* or the *"n-Body Problem"*, where *n* is a number equal to three or more. The three-body problem was encountered when Newton and others wanted to investigate the Sun-Earth-Moon system with the gravitational forces of all three taken into account. The solution to this problem turned out to be such a big deal even in later years that in 1887 Sweden's King Oscar II (1829-1907) announced a prize for anyone who could solve it. Extending from the work of German mathematician Heinrich Bruns (1848-1919), the French math and physics genius, Henry Poincaré (1854-1912) won the prize, for *not* solving the problem, but for mathematically proving that the three-body system was, in fact, practically unsolvable! After battling the problem for so long, he reported that the three-body problem for the Sun-Earth-Moon system, for example, produced orbits *"so tangled that I cannot even begin to draw them."* The other very important finding of his was the dependence of the outcome of *n*-body systems to their initial conditions. He wrote: *"It may happen that small differences in the initial positions may lead to enormous differences in the final phenomena. Prediction becomes impossible."* (4, 5) The findings and ideas of Poincaré, which were included in his "solution", later led to the discovery of a new chapter in science called the *"Chaos Theory"*, which rightfully entitles him to be called *"The Grandfather of Chaos Theory"*.

Fast forward to the second half of the twentieth century, 1961 to be exact. Although several scientists had been working on the three-body problem and on Poincaré's ideas, it was not until Edward Lorenz (1917-2008), an American meteorologist mathematician at MIT, pioneered the establishment of Chaos as a theory, as well as a new branch of mathematics. Before getting to Ed Lorenz's story though, I have to add a related side note here: In addition to the bright minds, one factor which played a pivotal role in the development of the theory of Chaos was the development and availability of high-speed digital computers with large calculation capabilities. Solving the n-body system equations, which involved numerous repetitions of solving one equation and using the results in the next by hand, turned out to be so tedious that it had become a limiting factor, and therefore, the new and evolving electronic computer technology was a really powerful and determining tool in the arsenal of the more recent investigators.

Successful weather prediction has always been the Holy Grail of meteorologists. This is because the weather plays some role in almost whatever we do. And it gets increasingly more important when it comes to large-scale activities such as sports, commerce, military, travel, shipments, *etc.* So, when the newer generation of electronic computers started to emerge during the 1950's, meteorologists were among happy campers because (as we all may already know) weather predictions, especially for periods of more than a few days, always proved to be very inaccurate, or mixed at the best. That's why Ed Lorenz had decided to use his expertise in mathematics to develop improved weather models for more accurate predictions. As a part of this process, he decided to test his models on a newly delivered computer at the MIT by feeding it several months' worth of modeling data. The models were *deterministic* differential equations of the same types used in Newton's Laws of Motion. Betting on the accuracy and efficiency of his computer, and the deterministic nature of the equations, he hoped to get nothing but consistent and reproducible results, and as such, it should not be to anyone's surprise that he was both shocked and disappointed when what his comp spat out at him was far from expectation. Instead of getting the same reproducible weather model, each time he plugged in the same initial numbers, out came a different one! As a savvy researcher, he double checked everything including the "sanity" of his computer and rerunning the program several times. Everything checked. At a point in time when a sharp, meticulous, and objective mind separates itself from a not-so-much one, Lorenz decided to look at his numbers. And there he got his answer: To save time, he had rounded off the numbers that originally contained 6 decimal places (DPs) to numbers with 3 DPs while the computer was still calculating based on 6 DPs. For example (*my* example not his), 1.023123 was rounded off to 1.023, as the contribution of the remaining "0.000123" was not expected to be of significance. This is both an allowed and usual a practice in science and that's why the seasoned mathematician did it and that's why he was sort of irritated when he got the "off" results. So, if a seemingly insignificant change in the starting numbers could produce significant changes in the outcome of the experiments (weather models in this case), then Ed Lorenz had arrived at, and proved right, what Henry Poincaré had proposed about three quarters of a century earlier: The hypersensitivity of *some systems* to their initial conditions (6). So, if we could call Poincaré the granddaddy of chaos, then we definitely could call Lorenz "*The Father of Chaos Theory*".

Now let's see what I mean by "some systems" in the last paragraph and what the "Chaos Theory" itself is anyway: By "some systems" I mean what is known in physics as "*Dynamical Systems*". Simply put, dynamical systems are those that change over time and that are sensitive to their initial conditions. The movement of ocean water, fluctuations of the stock market, patterns of traffic jams, movement of billiard balls on a pool table, and of course the weather, are examples of dynamical systems. It is in these systems that prediction of a future event, by using its initial condition data and having the right formulae, *could be* possible. But let me add also that "could be" is definitely not the same as "will be". This is beautifully done in the case of the two-body movements in the solar system and by the use of Newton's Laws of Motion, his gravitational attraction rules, and the differential equations he and Leibniz developed. This technique, though, would not work for three- and *n*-body systems as described above.

Now what about the Chaos Theory and what it says? First just remember that this theory holds only in dynamical systems. For a system to get "chaotic" it has to be a dynamical one first. The findings of investigators from Poincaré to Lorenz on the unpredictability of the n-body dynamical systems led the American mathematicians James Yorke and T.Y. Li to coin the term *"Chaos"* for this phenomenon in 1975, and thus, the related theory has been known as the *Chaos Theory* (7). Simply stated, the theory is a proposition on the behavior of dynamical systems: The change in a dynamical system at any future time, t, is highly sensitive to even minute variations in its initial conditions (*IC*) at time zero (t_0) and cannot be precisely predicted due to the lack of perfect precision in the *IC* measurements. Also, the precision of any prediction at time t is inversely proportional to the time difference, $t - t_0$, meaning the longer the $t - t_0$, the lower the precision.

What I have talked about so far in this chapter may now lead to this question: "If deterministic differential equations are used to calculate the outcome of a dynamical event, and when we feed the equations with real data, why should we come out with chaotic results?" The answer is in our inability to *reproducibly* make *100% accurate* measurements (the data) *and* the inability of our processors (such as computers) to *reproducibly* process those data. These inabilities, coupled with the nature of dynamical systems described in the last paragraph, make Chaos *inevitable*.

Now this: It has been the belief in this "inevitability" that leads some of us to reject Causal Determinism, on the grounds that occurrences of all Events (of any type, from cosmic to those of our daily lives) are chaotic, thus unpredictable, and therefore, non-deterministic! For example, Peter Dizikes wrote in one of the 2011 issues of the *MIT Technology Review*: *"Half a century ago, Edward Lorenz .... overthrew the idea of the clockwork universe with his ground-breaking research on chaos."* (8)

My answer to this kind of belief is this: Events happen and life (in its universal sense) goes on. There is only *one* way in which Events could happen, at least in *this* Universe, and that's the way they do happen. That is, all possibilities for something to occur will boil down to one and only one possibility and that's the one that *does* occur. Stating in another way, an "occurred" Event is *the* only single actuality from a number of potentialities. The argument of Chaos is due to the lack of our ability to precisely predict the future. But the World does not care whether or not we can predict the future. It does its own work and goes through one and only one channel, the "causally determined" channel. In fact, Ed Lorenz himself once wrote *"Chaos: When the present determines the future, but the approximate present does not approximately determine the future."* (9) To me, the first part of this statement (before the comma) clearly confirms the deterministic nature of the Universe by confirming the validity of the Cause-and-Effect principle. The second part (after the comma), however, is irrelevant because in actuality there is no such a thing as *"approximate present"*. The present is either "0" or "1". What Lorenz must have meant was that our inability in making 100% accurate *and* reproducible measurements make the present "approximate". In other words, what Lorenz calls "approximate" is, in fact, *our* approximate knowledge of the present due to the fact that our measurements and the function of our calculating instruments are approximate, and as such, are not, and could not be, 100% accurate. Otherwise, the present has only one single facet and that's what that actually happens, and therefore, *is*. The future is always precisely determined. We just can't know it!

REFERENCES

1. Newton I, Axioms or Laws of Motion, In: *Philosophiæ Naturalis Principia Mathematica*, 1: 19, 1729.
2. Ogg JM and Gradstein FM, *A Geologic Time Scale*, Cambridge University Press, 2004, ISBN 0-521-78142-6.
3. Elert E, Giant Asteroid Impact Dated-Precisely- to Dinausors' End, *Pop Sci*, February 2013.
4. Chenciner A, Poincaré and the Three-Body Problem, In: *Progress in Mathematical Physics*, Springer, Volume 67, 2014, pp. 51-149.
5. See also: http://home.earthlink.net/~srrobin/chaos.html
6. Lorenz EN, Deterministic Nonperiodic Flow, *J Atm Sci*, 20 (2): 130-141, 1963. DOI: 10.1175/1520-0469(1963)020<0130:DNF>2.0.CO;2
7. Li TY and York JA, Period Three Implies Chaos, *Am Math Mont*, 82(10): 985-982, 1975.
8. Dizikes P, When the Butterfly Effect Took Flight, *MIT News Magazine*, February 2011. URL: https://www.technologyreview.com/s/422809/when-the-butterfly-effect-took-flight/
9. Danforth CM, Chaos in an Atmosphere Hanging on a Wall, In: *Mathematics of Planet Earth, 2013*.

CHAPTER 12

A Strange Science

"It is safe to say that nobody understands quantum mechanics."

RICHARD FEYNMAN (1918-1988),
PHYSICIST, NOBEL LAUREATE

BY THE END OF THE nineteenth century, physicists were happy scientists. They believed they knew most of the things they needed to know to be able to solve almost any major problem related to the physical aspects of the Universe. The laws motion and gravity of Isaac Newton (Chapter 11) could, to a very high degree of certainty, address any issues related to motion and in combination with the improving calculus, the concept of "Rational Mechanics" had gained both respect and wide-spread applicability (*1*). Thermodynamics (the physics of heat, temperature, work, energy, and their relationship) was at the top of its evolution as a major branch of physics. This important subject owed this significant development to the works of Julius Robert von Mayer (1814-1878), James Prescott Joule (1818-1889), Sadi Carnot (1796-1832), and William Thomson (Lord Kelvin, 1824-1907) among others (*2*). The concept of electromagnetism and its relation to the wave nature of light, itself previously introduced by

Christiaan Huygens (1629-1695), was significantly developed by James Clerk Maxwell (1831-1879) making important contributions to optics and other areas of physics and science in general (3).

It was at the peak of this "physical euphoria" (and probably the related scientific arrogance) that Nature decided to tickle and tease the brains of physicists one more time. And she did that by leading them to some new observations and experimental puzzles which were not solvable through the accumulated knowledge of the classical physics: Discovered first in 1896 by Henri Becquerel (1852-1908), Marie (1867-1934) and Pierre (1859-1906) Curie noted an unusual radiation by a certain type of matter which countered what was known about the indestructible nature of atoms (4). The Curies then coined the term *"radioactivity"* for this observation. Based on these observations, and along with the discovery of the electron in 1897 by J.J. Thomson (1856-1940), Ernest Rutherford (1871-1937) and his student Frederick Soddy (1877-1956) proposed a new model for atomic structure in 1911 which consisted of a dense positively charged nucleus surrounded by negatively charged electrons. This would have been quite a breakthrough except that according to the classical physics, this structure was not stable: The negatively charged electrons and the positively charged nuclei would eventually collide and annihilate due to the mutual electromagnetic attraction of opposite charges. This, of course, showed one of the shortcomings of the classical mechanics.

Another failure of the classical physics in explaining experimental findings was demonstrated by Albert Michelson (1852-1931) and Edward Morley (1838-1923) at Case Western Reserve University in Cleveland, Ohio, through the so-called Michelson-Morley Experiment (MME). Until that time, it had been postulated that light propagated in space as waves (which light was thought of to be) and through a stationary medium called the "luminiferous ether" or light-bearing ether. Without the ether, it was believed, light could not propagate in space. By elaborately performing the MME in 1887, Michelson and Morley showed that the luminiferous, or any other medium, did not exist, thus indicating that light was, in fact, capable of travelling in vacuum space all by itself (5).

But, although the evolution of science is a continuum of contributions from a countless number of scientists and within a very long history, perhaps two of the more famous cases that not only invalidated the "universality" of the classical physics but also led to the "Physics Revolution" of the twentieth century, were Max Planck's explanation of the Blackbody Radiation (6) and Einstein's explanation of the Photoelectric Effect (7, 8). In physics, a blackbody (BB) is an ideal object that completely absorbs all the energy that it has been irradiated with, without any scattering (reflection) or re-emission. In practice, the closest models to the ideal BBs are made as thick-walled boxes with a matt black color and with a tiny hole in one of the walls which is theoretically the only outlet of energy and through which the BB's emissions are recorded and studied. At thermal equilibrium (that is, when temperature is the same all over the body) the BB emits a spectrum of light at the frequencies related to the BB's temperature. This radiation is *"called blackbody radiation"*. The spectrum includes light from infrared (IR) to ultraviolet (UV) frequencies (or wavelengths) and colors from red to yellow to a brilliant and intense white. When the intensity of the radiated light is plotted (or graphed) against its wavelengths, the BB radiation appears as almost bell-shaped curves (Note: wavelength is the inverse of frequency, or mathematically, one divided by frequency). The BB radiation was first introduced by Gustav Kirchhoff (1824-1887) in 1860 but was studied extensively by a number of scientists who all found a nagging problem with this experiment: When calculations of classical physics were used to *predict* the intensity (or the bell-shaped curve) of radiation at short wavelengths and at high temperature, the curve shot up to infinite values. As mentioned, this was observed at short wavelengths (or high frequencies) and in the in the UV radiation range. This meant that there would be an *infinite* amount of energy radiating out of the BB which was, of course, against the laws of Nature. This problem has been known in physics as the *"Ultraviolet Catastrophe"*. Then in 1900, the German theoretical physicist, Max Planck (1858-1947) showed that by assuming discrete values for the radiated energies of the BB (instead of a continuum of values used in the classical physics) the Ultraviolet Catastrophe could be avoided. Planck's hypothesis was also supported by that of the great Austrian physicist and philosopher, Ludwig Boltzmann (1844-1906) who stated in 1877 that the energy states of a physical system could be discrete. Indeed, assigning whole and discrete values for energy led to a beautiful agreement between the experimental data and Planck's calculated results on BB radiation patterns. The UV Catastrophe could be avoided and Planck later suggested that light and electromagnetic radiation were, in fact, emitted as discrete "packets" of energy which he called *"quanta"*. This novel and revolutionary proposition opened the gates of human knowledge to a whole new world of science later to be known as *Quantum Mechanics* (9).

The second fateful contribution towards the establishment of quantum mechanics was made by the genius of Albert Einstein and by his solving of the *Photoelectric Effect* problem (7). The photoelectric effect (PE) is a process in which, upon impinging on some materials (such as a metallic surface), light ejects electrons from that material. It is widely used in the industry with simple examples being automatic doors and remote controls. The classical electromagnetic theory, which considered light to be of a continuous wave nature, predicted that electrons were ejected as a result of energy transfer from light in a light intensity-dependent manner. This meant that changes in the intensity (or brightness) of light would proportionally change the rate of electron ejection. Experimental results, however, did not show any intensity-ejection rate correlation. Rather, it was observed that electron ejection was directly proportional to the frequency of the incoming light such that if the frequency was below a certain level, no electrons could be extracted regardless of the brightness of the light and the duration of the irradiation. Through consideration of Planck's hypothesis on the blackbody radiation (6), Einstein proposed (7) in 1905 that light was not a propagation of waves through space but rather it was particulate packages of energy with discrete frequencies of integer values. Einstein's proposition explained why the rate of electron ejection was independent of light intensity and why even extended periods of irradiation could not result in electron ejection if the light frequency was below a certain level.[1] For these historical achievements, Max Planck and Albert Einstein were awarded the Nobel Prize in physics in 1918 and 1921, respectively.

Although there are many aspects of physics that relate to quantum theory, I wish to limit the discussion here to that of the atomic structure as it relates to the main subject of this book. As mentioned above, the atomic structure of Rutherford which was based on the classical physics, suffered the major shortcoming of instability. This and another deficiency, the inability to explain the experimental results from the emission spectra of different atomic structures, pointed to the weakness of this model. Utilizing Planck's and Einstein's hypotheses on the quantization of energy (the discrete-package nature of energy and light), Danish physicist Niels Bohr proposed in 1913 that electron's energy levels in the "Solar System" model of Rutherford were quantized and that electrons were allowed to reside in only *one* certain orbit (energy level) at a time, and therefore, their *continuous* spiral fall into the nucleus was forbidden (*10*).[2] Although Bohr's model did solve the instability problem and could predict the emission spectral lines of hydrogen atom (a 1-electron system), it could not explain the spectral lines of *multi*-electron atoms.[3]

In the year 1924, the French Physicist Louis de Broglie (1892-1987, pronounced "Lui Dibroy"), came up with a hypothesis that turned out to be not only revolutionary but one of the major and fundamental principles in quantum mechanics. According to de Broglie's hypothesis, moving matter (including the electron) shows a wave-like behavior (later, this came to be known as the *"wave-particle duality of matter"*). Interestingly, he postulated this as a graduate student and as part of his Doctorate dissertation in 1924 (*11*). Even more interesting was the fact that the correctness of his postulate was shown experimentally by two American physicists, Clinton Davisson (1881-1958) and Lester Germer (1896-1971) in 1927, locking the1929 Nobel Prize in physics for Monsieur Louis.

The Bohr's model of the atom being not a perfect one, and de Broglie's wave-particle duality concept now published, another bright and highly capable of "thinking-out-of-the-box" mind, took note. The Austrian physicist, Erwin SchrÖdinger, wondered what would happen if, in the mathematical modeling of the atomic structure, the electron in the Bohr's model was treated as a wave. He went to work and in 1926 published the Schrödinger equation which defines electron as a wave rather than a point-like particle (*12*). Schrödinger's approach could remove the shortcomings of the Bohr's model and explain (or predict) spectral results for *multi*-electron atoms. As it is one of the more important findings in quantum mechanics, let's see what a Schrödinger equation is anyway. And to avoid redundancies, it may be not a bad idea to acquaint ourselves with this piece of "scientific art" through the following stepwise definitions:

1. The Schrödinger equation describes variations in the quantum states of a quantum system with respect to time and through solving of the "Wave Function" of that system.
2. A "quantum state" refers to the state of isolated quantum systems and provide a probability distribution for the value of each possible measurement on that system.
3. A "quantum system" is a part of the Universe that is under quantum mechanical analysis based on the wave-particle duality of

that system. Everything out of the system is referred to as the "Environment" which is studied for its effects on the System.
4. A Wave Function provides the *probabilities* for the possible results of measurements made on the quantum system.

A simple example of the application of the Schrödinger equation is the structure prediction for the simplest of atoms, hydrogen. The equation (or the wave function) may be solved to predict the possible points in space (or the quantum states) where there is a probability for the single-electron of hydrogen (or the quantum system) to exist around the atom's nucleus.

Schrödinger further suggested that the square of the wave function would yield the density of electrons in any point in space. (In mathematics, square of anything means that "thing" to its second power as square of 2 is $2^2 = 2 \times 2 = 4$). In the same year (1926), the German physicist and mathematician, Max Born (1882-1970) corrected Schrödinger's interpretation by stating that the square of the wave function gives the *probability density* of an electron and not it's *physical* density. Born's hypothesis, which turned out to be right, means that the square of the wave function represents the probability of finding an electron in any particular quantum state such as energy, momentum, or position, at any particular time. (In physics, momentum of an object is its mass multiplied by its velocity). In short, the wave function and Schrödinger equation provide a probabilistic (as opposed to deterministic) picture of the microscopic and subatomic world which, at least in the first glance, may contrast the more familiar classical and deterministic Newtonian observations of the macroscopic world.

Speaking of "probability", the mention of one more very important topic of the quantum theory may be in order: In 1927, another

German theoretical physicist and one of the major pioneers of quantum physics, Werner Heisenberg (1901-1976) published a paper on his findings about a new concept. During earlier years, and in collaboration with Max Born and Pascual Jordan (1902-1980), Heisenberg had been able to develop a new kind of mathematical procedure called "Matrix" through which he also developed a new formulation of quantum mechanics, called *"Matrix Mechanics"*. Combining the matrix approach with other findings in quantum physics, he asserted in a 1927 paper that there was a fundamental limit to the accuracy with which certain pairs of physical properties of a particle, such as momentum and position, could be measured at the same time. In other words, the more precisely the momentum of a particle is known, the less accurately its position may be measured and *vice versa*. This is known as the *"Heisenberg Uncertainty Principle"* for which Heisenberg was awarded the Nobel Prize in physics in 1932 (*13*). A thought experiment he used to illuminate his point was something like this: Using a light microscope, let's assume that you want to perform an experiment to "see" the position of an electron and measure its velocity while the electron is still under the microscope. This means two observations (or measurements) at the same time. For you to be able to see the electron, the light photons from the microscope's lamp should collide with the electron and reflect off of it and into your eyes. But the moment the microscope's light photons hit the electron, they change the electron's velocity (just like two balls collide on a pool table), and thereby, alter its momentum (as momentum is the product of mass times velocity). And as such, the simultaneous making of these two measurements would not be possible.

The Uncertainty Principle is one of the cornerstones of modern physics although some recent work is in progress to check the degree of its validity (*14*).

The Double-Slit Experiment

When it came to the nature of light, the 18th- and 19th-Century scientists were divided into two groups: A major group who believed in Isaac Newton's "corpuscular" (or particle-like) character of light, and a minor group who thought of light as a wave. In 1801, Thomas Young (1773-1829) performed an experiment which at the time showed the validity of the claim of the "Wave Group". The experiment used a light source, a plane to serve as a screen, and a plate containing a tiny hole placed in between the light source and the screen. Young showed that when light passed through the hole, it split and then recombined after the passage to produce an alternatively light and dark striped pattern on the screen. This pattern was called an *"Interference Pattern"* or a *"Diffraction Pattern"*. Since this was a known characteristic of interfering waves, like ripples on the surface of a pond, Young was able to prove that light propagated as waves. The bright and dark stripes formed when waves of light coming off of the hole were in-phase (bright, amplifying one another) or out-of-phase (dark, destructing each other), respectively. This was the belief until the 20th Century, the year 1923 to be exact, when the American physicist, Arthur Compton (1892-1962), observed in his experiment that light, as X-rays, bounced off of electrons, again just like the colliding balls on a pool table. Needless to say, this was a characteristic behavior of particles. And the take home message, if the results of these experiments were valid (and there was no reason to think otherwise), was that light had a dual wave-particle character. But wait, there is more!

The experiment was later repeated by other scientists and with slits instead of holes. These experiments are, therefore, given the generic name *"Double-Slit (DS)"* experiments. Figures 1 shows a simplified diagram of the DS experiment (a) and an example of a diffraction pattern (b).

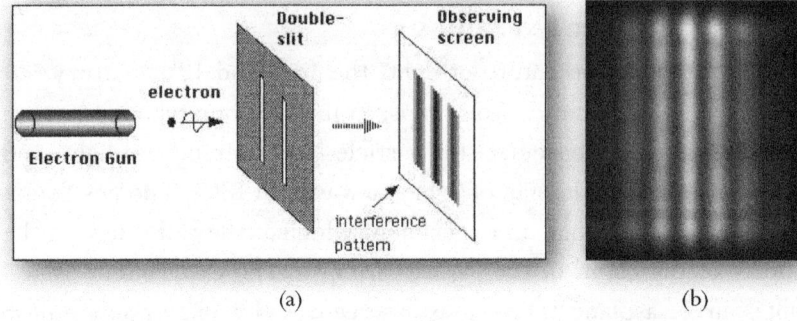

(a) (b)

Figure 1. A simplified diagram of the double-slit experimental set-up (a) and a typical diffraction (or interference) pattern as displayed on the screen (b). While an electron (that is a particle) is shown to be used in (a), photons of light could also be used as discussed in the text. In the case of photons, a light source would replace the electron gun. A no-diffraction pattern would have only two of these vertically parallel lines. Figure credit.[4]

Also, in addition to light, the DS experiments were carried out with particles such as electrons, protons, atoms, and even molecules (by now you should be able to know the differences among these groups of particles if you recall our previous chapters). And in addition to performing experiments with groups of particles, they were done with single particles and single photons passing through slits one at a time (and remember photons are "packets" of light energy so they could be considered particles of light). This means, instead of releasing a whole bunch of particles or photons through the slits, they were "fired" one at a time, but for quite a number of times, and the patterns of the collisions with the screen were recorded. Before we go further, though, I would like to draw your attention to something about a *particle* DS experiment: If we shoot particles (golf balls, marbles, electrons, photons, *etc.*) through a pair of slits, we would expect to see a particle-characteristic pattern on the screen: After randomly passing through the slits at a 50:50 probability and accumulating on the screen, the particles would be expected to produce two parallel lines. But when the experiments were actually done, the results were totally unexpected: Both light photons and particles hit the screen one by one but accumulated to gradually develop exactly the same vertical stripes of the *interference* pattern which had been observed when the light and particles were fired continuously and behaved as waves. The one-at-a-time firing of the particles eventually showed *several* parallel stripes and not just two!

After repetitions of these experiments showed that results were indeed reproducible, the investigators could draw only one conclusion: Light was also particle and particles were also light, or, light and matter could be considered both waves *and* particles.

While the patterns resulted from the "continuous firing" experiments were expected (that is, light and particles behaved as waves and waves went through both slits at the same time and interfered with each other on the other side), an explanation for the observation of the pattern when light and particles were fired one at a time, was that each single light photon or each single particle (such as electrons) went through *both* slits at the same time! So, to see how the tiny puzzlers did that, the head-scratching, baffled and dazzled investigators installed detectors at the entrance of one of the slits in the single-shot experiments. If the photon or particle passed through that slit, they could be detected, and if they did not, they must have passed through the other slit. "Yesss!" they said, "that must do it, we're too smart to be intimidated by a few of lowly particles." Well, not smart enough, I'm afraid: When the experiments were "detected", the photons and particles behaved as particles, went through either one slit or the other, and produced a non-interference pattern, that is, two parallel stripes as you would expect when particles behave like particles. No more wavy behavior (*15*). Still, when the detectors were off, particles again behaved as waves and produced the interference patterns on the screen.

The *detected* double-slit experiments are called "Which-Path" experiments because the path of the photons and particles could be identified by using the detectors.

After some more head scratching, the researchers thought "aha, this was because the detectors were placed before the slits and the particles "saw" them, so let's hide the detectors behind the slits." (The method is now known as the "Delayed-Choice" experiment because the identification of the path "choice" of the particles is delayed to after they pass the slits). So, they did, and results were the same. Particles refused to reveal their wavy nature when somebody, or some "thing", watched them and no interference pattern were observed. The little things were smarter than what they were given credit for. This meant only one thing: Observation (such as detection or measurement) collapsed the outcome from "wave-particle duality" to a "particle-only" singularity.[5]

Thanks to the resilient spirit of physicists, the researchers designed yet another, a bit more sophisticated, experiment (**Please Note:** If you don't feel like you are scientifically and experimentally inclined, please skip the experimental details and go to the last paragraph of this section and carry on from there. You'll be just as fine.): This time, they thought maybe separating the detected group from the screen-hitting group may do the trick. Maybe, the particles would not "smell" the detectors and play as they would without them. That is, if they are split into pairs of "twins", even while their twins are detected, they would not find out and would produce the interference (wave) patterns. So, some kind of "splitter" was placed after the two slits so when the light particles exited each slit, they would be re-split in two "twin" entities (in quantum physics, these twins are called "entangled" particles). So, now we have a total of four beams (*i.e.*, two twins) that would be divided into two couples. One couple was sent to the screen as usual, to reveal their pattern of impact (interference or otherwise) and the other was sent through detectors which, in turn, would tell you which slit each singly fired particle or photon came through. Unbelievably, and to everyone's absolute amazement, the results were the same as before. The separated entangled twins somehow were still informationally in-touch because even the "no-detector" group still would not produce the interference patterns. But listen to this, when the detectors were turned off, that is, *no observation*, production of the interference patterns resumed. This procedure is called "Delayed-Choice Quantum Eraser Experiment" because one could turn off the detectors at will, and thus, erase the process of observation (16).

The conclusion of the experiments: Once the experimenters were aware of which one of the two slits the particles went through, the particles stopped behaving as waves and the wave-characteristic interference patterns disappeared. English translation: Consciousness creates the reality. Spooky.[6]

THE COPENHAGEN INTERPRETATION

I can say with a good degree of confidence that rarely are there areas in science that have as much depth and vastness as does quantum physics. I can even go a bit farther and call it an "Intellectual Abyss". These very characters have also led to enormous difficulties in a perfect understanding and interpretation of this area of science. These difficulties, though, have not been able to keep the curiously adventurous human scientist from at least attempting to understand the quantum theory. This has been demonstrated by quite a few Nobel prizes, awarded to those who have offered their contribution by proposing interpretations of this strange yet fascinating chapter of science.

One of the most famous interpretations of the quantum theory (QT) is known as the Copenhagen interpretation proposed in the mid 1920's by Neils Bohr and Werner Heisenberg. The name is said to have been given to this interpretation by Heisenberg, in or around 1955, and as a tribute to the birthplace of Bohr, the Danish capital Copenhagen (17).

To make the "mental digestion" of the interpretation a bit easier, let me talk about some terms used its definition. The term "measurement" needs no clarification but when it comes to the QT, everything may have a different meaning. Here, measurement and "observation" may be the same. And the way I convinced myself about this is that when we are "observing" some event, our brains are, in reality, evaluating that event in that the incoming information would be analyzed and screened against the brain's stored data to synthesize some kind of a conclusion. This process of screening, analyzing, and concluding is, in fact, a type of "measurement" as the latter word is an evaluation of new data against some previously acquired knowledge. Coming through the other end, anytime we are measuring something, we have to be observing it too. So, I use "measurement" and "observation" interchangeably in here. Another term is "physical system". A physical system is a part of the Universe within which an observation is being made. If you are looking through your living room window to see if it's raining in your backyard, your backyard is your "physical system". A "quantum state" is the state of isolated quantum systems and represents the probability distribution for the value of each possible measurement on that system. And finally, a "wave function" is (putting it in a very simplified way) the *"probability"* with which an observation results in one single state of a physical system to materialize.

According to the QT, for every system there may exist an infinite number of wave functions prior to the act of measurement. Quantum mechanics, therefore, is a *"predictive"* science. It can only *predict* the probability of a certain outcome of a measurement.

According to the Copenhagen interpretation of the QT, physical systems, in their quantum states, do not have exact and precise properties *prior* the act of measurement. They are only a series of *probabilities* of an outcome, each of which is called a "Wave Function". This state of simultaneous existence of probabilities is called "quantum superposition". The act of measurement or observation immediately causes the state of superposition to break down and *all* probabilities to reduce to only one which shows up as an outcome (or Event). This process of the reduction of all probabilities to only one possibility is referred to as *"Wave function Collapse"* (see the definition of wave function above). So, the Copenhagen interpretation of the quantum world, now explains the "weird" results of the double-slit experiments (albeit in its own terms): The act of "detection", which is a kind of measurement, collapsed the wave functions of the event of diffraction of light or matter particles (which was the result of their wave-like behavior) to only one, and caused them to behave like what they were supposed to be, particles. The particle-like behavior then produced the corresponding pattern of two parallel stripes. According to this interpretation, if the world is ruled by quantum mechanics, you would never know what's in the tea leaves until you actually make an observation. There is no reality until you're aware of it!

The collapse approach, therefore, proposes that the Universe is factually indeterminate. And as such, it would not be possible to predict what state a superposition will collapse into, and therefore, it is impossible to know the future, even if you have all the necessary information about the present.

Although I am sure things are somewhat clear by now, I would still like to refer to this famous saying that *"a picture is worth a thousand words"* and try to draw a mental picture of the Copenhagen interpretation for you to make sure all is clear about what we are looking at. And that's going to be the picture of a very famous yet mysterious feline, called the Schrödinger Cat.

The Schrödinger Cat

The Schrödinger Cat or Schrödinger Paradox is a thought experiment which was originally invented by the Austrian physicist, Erwin Schrödinger, the man who developed the Schrödinger wave equation that we touched on before (*18*). Interestingly, Schrödinger offered this thought experiment as a critique to the Copenhagen interpretation but it has actually become a frequently used yardstick for physicists to evaluate different interpretations of quantum mechanics. Before describing the experiment, let me refresh your memories about the topic of "Radioactive Half-Life". You may already know that a radioactive element, also called a radioactive isotope, is an unstable atom that spontaneously decays to new atoms called "daughter elements" plus energy in the form of some kind of radiation. A radioactive half-life, denoted as $t_{1/2}$ (and pronounced "tee-one-half), is the time period during which a given radioactive isotope decays to half of its original amount (or mass). The $t_{1/2}$ is isotope-specific and actually may be used as a fingerprint information to identify an unknown radioactive sample.

The set-up of the Schrödinger cat experiment consists of a sealable box containing a very small amount of a radioactive isotope with a decay $t_{1/2}$ of, say, one hour, a detector that picks up the radiation emitted by the radioactive decay, a glass flask containing cyanide poison, a hammer above, and pointed to, the flask, and of course, our snuggly feline, that I shall call Schroc (for <u>Schrö</u>dinger <u>C</u>at). After all components of the experiment, including Schroc, are in, the box is sealed, and left without any disturbance for 1 hour, that is, the $t_{1/2}$ of the radioisotope inside. The detector is connected to the hammer in a way that if it picked up a radiation from the decay of the radioactive isotope, the hammer would be released to swing down and break the flask, releasing the cyanide poison, which in turn, kills Schroc. From the definition of half-life above, it is readily apparent that after 1 hour, there is a 50% chance that our isotope would decay to emit the radiation which would release the hammer, and 50% chance that it would not. This means that after 1 hour, there is a 50:50 probability that Schroc is dead or alive. Now here comes the twist: According to the combination of Schrödinger wave equation, that gives equal probability to *all* the possible outcomes, and the Copenhagen interpretation, which considers observation to be the "trigger" for the commencement of any physical Event, prior to an observation, Schroc would be *both* dead *and* alive. But after an hour, once somebody opens the box and peeks into it, the reality immediately materializes and the observer would find either a dead Schroc or a living Schroc. It would be the very act of observation that finalizes the fate of the poor (or lucky) feline.

Schrödinger devised his cat experiment with two rationales in mind: 1. To show a way of connecting the microscopic quantum events (the atomic-level decay of the radioisotope) to the macroscopic events (the observation of an observer and the survival, or lack thereof, of Schroc), and 2. To demonstrate the irrationality of the Copenhagen interpretation. But, as mentioned before, the experiment has been one of the most frequently cited topics in quantum-related discussions as well as one of the standards to evaluate the validity of other interpretations of the quantum theory.

The reason for adding a chapter about quantum theory and the Copenhagen interpretation to this book was to include a viewpoint that is based on a probabilistic nature of our world. If the ultimate goal of this writing is to evaluate the possibilities for the existence of Freewill, leaving out an important chapter of science, which has critical attachments to metaphysical and ontological philosophies, would not have sounded like a logical approach. After the establishment of quantum theory, it was only natural for those with interest in the philosophy of science to be attracted to this fascinating field in the hopes of unlocking yet more of the mysteries of Nature and Life. When it comes to the topics of Determinism and Freewill, a very interesting aspect of quantum mechanics is that it has accommodated groups with opposite viewpoints. The discussions presented so far in this chapter point to a purely probabilistic, and thus nondeterministic, nature of the Universe. In fact, in one of the writings about Heisenberg's Uncertainty Principle, the author states (*19*):

> *"The principle effectively overturned in one fell swoop the whole doctrine of scientific determinism which had been implicitly assumed since Newton and Laplace in the 17th Century, and redefined the task of physics as the discovery of laws that will allow us to predict events UP TO THE LIMITS set by the uncertainty principle."* (Capitalization is from the original source.)

Should other alternatives not have been possible, I would have stopped writing this book immediately after reading that statement. But, as we shall find out in the next chapter, there are other contrasting interpretations which, at least as far as the rationale for writing this book is concerned, may show some light at the end of the tunnel for Determinism. So, let's continue our voyage to the other islands of thought and find out if they could offer firm grounds for us to disembark to or they are but a few square meters of swampland.

Notes

[1] These "packages of light" were named *"photons"* by the American physical chemist, Gilbert N. Lewis (1875-1946) in 1926.

[2] According to Rutherford's "Solar System" model for atomic structure electrons revolved around nucleus as planets around stars. This model lacked the stability consideration in that positive nuclei and negative electrons should eventually attract each other leading to a mutual destruction of the whole atom. For this to happen, electrons should go through a continuum of energy levels, and as such, would accept any energy values. In Bohr's model, which was based on quantum mechanical principles, however, electrons were allowed only to accept discrete energy levels and could not go through an energy continuum as a "falling" towards nucleus would require. As per Bohr's model, electrons could only move up in energy levels (an excited state) only if the absorb energy in discrete quantities from an outside source. Once the supply of that energy is discontinued, the electrons would return to their "home" orbital (the ground state). Under no circumstance are they allowed to fall onto the nucleus to destroy the atom.

[3] As described in Note 2 above, electrons could absorb energy (light) from an outside source to go to an excited state. When the electrons fall back to their ground state, they would emit back the energy they had absorbed in the form of light at one or more wavelengths. When fed into a spectroscope, these lights would show up as discrete lines which are characteristic of each atom and could be used as "fingerprints" to identify them.

[4] Credit for Figure 1:
(a) **Attribution:** By No machine-readable author provided. NekoJaNekoJa~commonswiki assumed (based on copyright claims).

[GFDL (http://www.gnu.org/copyleft/fdl.html), CC-BY-SA-3.0 (http://creativecommons.org/licenses/by-sa/3.0/) or CC BY-SA 2.5-2.0-1.0 (http://creativecommons.org/licenses/by-sa/2.5-2.0-1.0)], via Wikimedia Commons
Page URL: https://commons.wikimedia.org/wiki/File%3ADouble-slit.PNG
File URL: https://upload.wikimedia.org/wikipedia/commons/5/57/Double-slit.PNG

(b) *Photo of the Double-Slit Interference of the Sunlight,* **Attribution:** By Aleksandr Berdnikov (Own work) [CC BY-SA 4.0 (http://creative-commons.org/licenses/by-sa/4.0)], via Wikimedia Commons
Page URL: https://commons.wikimedia.org/wiki/File%3ADouble_slit_interference.png
File URL: https://upload.wikimedia.org/wikipedia/commons/c/c1/Double_slit_interference.png

[5]It is important not to confuse this "singularity", which means "a single possibility of occurrence", with the "Singularity" of the Big Bang which means a point of beginning out of which the Universe was born.

[6]If you need more explanation, or you are interested in more detailed discussions, about the Double-Slit (D-S) and the Delayed-Choice Quantum Eraser (D-CQE) experiments, you could see informative videos at the following sites:

DS: https://www.youtube.com/watch?v=U7Z_TIw9InA

D-CQE: https://www.youtube.com/watch?v=H6HLjpj4Nt4

REFERENCES

1. Taliaferro RC, *Rational Mechanics: The Classic Notre Dame Course*, Hahn A, Banchoff T, Crosson F, Eds., 2014.
2. Thomson W, *Mathematical and Physical Papers*, Cambridge University Press, 1: 232, 1882.
3. Nahin PJ, Maxwell's Grand Unification, *Spectrum*, 29 (3): 45, 1992. DOI: 10.1109/6.123329
4. Reid RW, *Marie Curie*, New American Library, pp. 61–63, 1974, ISBN 0-00-211539-5.
5. Michelson AA and Morley EW, On the Relative Motion of the Earth and the Luminiferous Ether, *Am J Sci*, 34: 333-345, 1887. DOI: 10.2475/ajs.s3-34.203.333
6. Planck, M, On the Law of Distribution of Energy in the Normal Spectrum, *Ann Phys*, 4 (3): 553, 1901.
7. Einstein A, On a Heuristic Point of View Concerning the Production and Transformation of Light, *Ann Phys*, 17: 132–148, 1905.
8. Galison P, Holton GJ, Schweber SS, *Einstein for the 21st Century: His Legacy in Science, Art, and Modern Culture*, Princeton University Press, pp. 161–164, 2008, ISBN 0-691-13520-7.
9. Kragh, H, *Quantum Generations: A History of Physics in the Twentieth Century*, Princeton University Press, 2002, ISBN 0-691-09552-3.
10. Bohr, N, On the Constitution of Atoms and Molecules. Part II: Systems Containing Only a Single Nucleus, *Phil Mag*, 26 (153): 476–502, 1913. DOI: 10.1080/14786441308634993
11. Greiner W, *Quantum Mechanics: An Introduction*, Springer, 2001, ISBN 3-540-67458-6.
12. Schrödinger E, An Undulatory Theory of the Mechanics of Atoms and Molecules, *Phys Rev*, 28 (6): 1049–1070. DOI: 10.1103/PhysRev.28.1049
13. Heisenberg W, Über den anschaulichen Inhalt der quantentheoretischen Kinematik und Mechanik (German: "On the Illustrative

Content of Qualitative Theoretical Kinematics and Mechanics"), *Zeit Phys, 43 (3–4): 172-198, 1927.*

14. https://www.utoronto.ca/news/u-t-scientists-cast-doubt-uncertainty-principle
15. Rae AIM, *Quantum Physics: Illusion or Reality?* Cambridge University Press. pp. 9–10, 2004, ISBN 1139455273.
16. Kim Y-H, et al., A Delayed "Choice" Quantum Eraser, *Phys Rev Lett,* 84: 1–5, 2000, Bibcode: 2000PhRvL..84....1K. DOI: 10.1103/PhysRevLett.84.1
17. Heisenberg W, The Development of the Interpretation of the Quantum Theory, In: *Niels Bohr and the Development of Physics,* Pauli W, Ed., Pergamon, pp. 12–29, 1955.
18. Schrödinger E, Die gegenwärtige Situation in der Quantenmechanik (German: "The Present Situation in Quantum Mechanics"), *Naturwissenschaften,* 23 (48): 807–812, 1935. DOI: 10.1007/BF01491891
19. Mastin L, Quantum Theory and the Uncertainty Principle: Quantum Tunneling and the Uncertainty Principle, *The Physics of the Universe,* 2009. URL: http://www.physicsoftheuniverse.com/topics_quantum_uncertainty.html

CHAPTER 13

The Synthesis

—∞—

"Experience teaches us no less clearly than reason, that men believe themselves free, simply because they are conscious of their actions, and unconscious of the causes whereby those actions are determined."

BARUCH SPINOZA IN *ETHICS*

IN THE LAST ELEVEN CHAPTERS I tried to put together the ingredients for the final synthesis of The Theory in a stepwise and systematic manner. The reason is that what I am talking about in this book has to do with the world we live in, sort of an analysis of the connectivity between us, our lives, our fates, and the physical phenomena from and through which we have come to exist. At the same time, I believe "stepwise and systematic" is the way in which our Universe has come to *be* and continues to *become*. So, if the subject of the discussion is a metaphysical one, then the set-up and conduct of the discussion itself should be based on the same pattern, stepwise and systematic.

The "Theory" referred to in the title of the book is by no means "*de novo*", and therefore, is not my invention. Perhaps I could say that it has existed for almost as long as the human's self-consciousness and intellectuality has. My rationale for attempting to re-introduce it in this book was the hope for a re-evaluation of it by both those who always have believed in it as well as those who never have. To me, such an attempt would be a winner either way: It may be able to give both groups just another tool to use for reinforcing their beliefs *for* or *against* the Theory, respectively. And yes, I did something else. I added a new name (or title) to describe the Theory. I added the new name *"No-Choice Theory"* to the old one, the *"Theory of Causal Determinism"*, and I should emphasize, not to replace the old one, of course, but to add to it. This was not an easy decision, though, as we humans do not like negative and limiting terms. We are always happier with pretty things, and sadly, sometimes even if they are not true or real. But I had to do it. I had to say it like what I thought it was. To me, if the world works with a causally deterministic mechanism, then we do not have any choice in changing anything, thereby the term (or the nickname) "No-Choice" for the theory of Causal Determinism. Furthermore, if I believed in a theory, especially through a scientific justification, and I wanted to share what I had learned with my readers, I had to be honest. Sure, our beliefs, findings, conclusions, *etc.*, could not be forced upon others, but in sharing them, one has to say them as they are. Just imagine what would have happened to our world if, for example, scientists were not honest in reporting their findings in any area like physics, chemistry, biology, which are the very foundations of engineering, pharmaceutics, and medicine and quite a few other important technologies. So, I firmly believe in intellectual honesty, and there you are having to face with this less-than-pretty title, the *No-Choice Theory*, and then some, reading this book about it!

Now let's do a quick review on what we have talked about so far. But before doing this review, let me remind you of the fact that Chapters 2-9 were written to emphasize on the orderly and stepwise nature of our world, the relatedness of its events and processes, and thus, the possibility of its working through a cause-and-effect mechanism. To this end, I believe a bottom-up demonstration of the development of "Structure" is of significant importance. This approach should be able to shed light on the fact that complexity is the product of stepwise combination and recombination processes that originate from simplicity and that Structure and the nature of its constituent elements (which also cause a "Universal Interaction" among everything) are the only determining factors in the development of effects, or what we may collectively call "Events".

Going back to our previous chapters and starting from the very beginning of it all, we talked about the Big Bang theory in Chapter 2. This scientifically well-supported theory explains the birth of our Universe and production of the first two elements of the Periodic Table, hydrogen and helium. With all of its (relative) structural simplicity, the atom of hydrogen shows an important aspect of Nature in that it was born out of a seemingly chaotic situation: Formation of hydrogen typifies the organization and order implied in natural processes. This "organization and order" is dictated by the laws of Nature, in this case the attraction, and the mutual cancelling out, of opposite electrical charges, and the allowance of only specific parts of space, called orbitals, for the electrons to exist. Electrons and protons have opposite charges, and therefore, could co-exist to build an atom. On the other hand, the energy levels of atomic orbitals are discrete integer values, which in hydrogen, put the electron at a well-defined distance from the nucleus.

There are other natural laws of physics too that, in unison, have led to the creation of our Universe: Movement of electrically charged particles, for instance, produces magnetic fields, or masses of matter warp spacetime (1) to create the force of gravity, and many other solid and unchangeable laws. And at least in this Universe, these laws are general and encompassing. That's why all hydrogen atoms are identical, all electrons are identical, and all water molecules are identical, in every physical aspect of their existence.

Chapter 3 talked about the make and electronic arrangement of atoms, the building blocks of the macroscopic world, and about the systematic geneses of higher atoms past hydrogen. Again, "organization" and "order" in the stepwise development of the world was shown to be the rule of the game. In Chapter 4 we learned how in yet another step of cosmic development, atoms could come together and make molecules. It was shown there that reacting atoms have to meet strict requirements to be able to form molecules. The information covered in these chapters is meant to demonstrate the fact that the *behavior* of each and every atom and molecule, or what we call the chemical and physical properties of any and every type of matter, is strictly determined by the electronic configuration of its constituting atoms and the overall atomic structures. And if, at a macroscopic scale, our material Universe is composed of atoms, it should be easy to see the importance of the overall interactions among all of them, which is based on the properties of each individual atom, on the ultimate outcome of events at each given point in time.

Chapter 5 discussed the different types of three-dimensional structures of polyatomic molecules. The highlight of this chapter was the relationship between the primary structures of molecules and their molecular shape which, in turn, is another factor in determining the properties and functions of any given molecule. The role and the effects of the environmental (or ambient) conditions in the formation of molecules was discussed in Chapter 6. There, we learned that in addition to the properties of the molecule-forming atoms, the very conditions in which molecules are born, would also be a determining factor.

After getting familiarized with atomic and molecular formation processes and the rules that conduct these processes, we moved to Chapter 7 where we reviewed the molecular machinery that produces microbes, plants, and animals, or what we could call the "Gene Machine". In addition to the act of "production", this amazing machine also "reproduces" the species in a delicate yet resilient process by recording and transferring hereditary information from parent to offspring generations.

Chapter 8 took us to the domain of structures and what they can do in determining the properties and functions of molecules such as the ones that form brains, and thereby, personalities and individual characters, as we talked about in Chapter 9. Chapter 10 was added as a brief refresher on some different theories of Determinism for those who were already familiar with the subject as well as being a didactic chapter for those who were new to these topics.

Finally, I added chapters 11 and 12, because at least by some of the readers, Chaos and Quantum theories might have been taken as counterarguments to the thesis of Determinism, and therefore, to what is meant to be the final conclusion of this book. And I perfectly understand such a way of thinking. From that point of view, it would be only natural to ask: "How could it be possible to have a determined world when events could happen chaotically and probabilistically, as may be suggested by these two theories?" Both Chaos and Quantum theories are based on valid scientific principles, and as such, any student of natural sciences finds no way but accepting them. But let's see if it would be possible to develop a "compromising" theory which is capable of interpreting a deterministic Universe in terms of these two theories. And in that hope, let's start the Synthesis.

As the first step, I need to draw your attention to a difference: The difference between *"our ability to predict future events"* and *"the events that actually happen in the future"*, and the understanding that these two are *not* the same. Frequently in my screening of the articles, notes, commentaries, *etc.*, in various sources, I find statements about "our inability to predict the future" because the Chaos Theory says the world events occur chaotically. Or, "future is absolutely beyond our ability to predict it" due to the Uncertainty Principle and the probabilistic nature of the world according to the Quantum Theory and the Copenhagen interpretation. One example of these was the statement shown at the end of Chapter 12 which was quoted from a description of the Heisenberg's Uncertainty Principle (see Chapter 12 and reference 19 therein) but there are other examples too. Now the funny thing is, they are right but only about certain aspects of the world's workings and not about all of them. I shall come back to this later on in this chapter when we revisit Chaos and Quantum principles. For right now, let's re-enter the discussion from another angle and look at the world through a hypothetical "window of law and order." For whatever reason (that is out of the scope of this book) and to the best of our knowledge, the Big Bang did occur and is well supported by both observational evidences and mathematical calculations. With the exclusion of the first 5.39 x 10^{-44} seconds of the Big Bang (that is, 0.0000000000000000000000000000000000000000539 seconds, called the Planck time), during which we as yet have no idea what happened, we know that things came together in an orderly manner (we'll have more on this "orderly manner" statement in the quantum section later in this chapter): The forces that were needed to crank up the formation of the material world were born, subatomic particles came together to make hydrogen, the grandmother of all other atoms which later made us and everything that we can see, hear, taste, smell, and touch. To refresh your memory, just remember it was in the highly energetic bellies of stars that hydrogen atoms fused together to make the second element of the Periodic Table, helium. Later on, and under increasingly more forceful star-core conditions, carbon and other heavier elements formed, which became the parents of molecules of every kind, including those that started the symphony of the biological life. Now let's stop here and think about the answer to this question: "When thinking about the vastness of the

Universe, the enormous number of the things (or more correctly, particles) that are contained in it, and the unimaginable physical dimensions that measure its volume, is it not just *convenient* to think of it as a discontinuous and "sectional" system?" I think the answer, at least from most of us, would be a resounding "Yes." "Of course the answer is yes", one might say, "don't you see that clouds are clouds, birds do what birds do, horses are horses, plants do their things, galaxies are spinning in faraway parts of space and have nothing to do with us, water runs downhill, and we humans live our own lives? Where is that "universal connectivity? Of course it is a sectional world! After all, what could a few atoms of carbon, oxygen, or iron, made some 13-something billion years ago have anything to do with me, who am living my life now?" Well, the fellow who asks those questions is, by no means, alone. There are millions of us, of almost any walk of life, who may think that way. The appearance of things makes it so easy to either forget, neglect, reject, or even downright deny, the possibilities of a "connectedness" that may exist among every Thing and every Event that, in unison, make the whole of our World.

In his logical way of thinking, Georges Lemaitre mentally rolled back the tape of the universal expansion and arrived at the now-well-supported model for the creation of the Universe called the Big Bang. With no claim of wanting to do such revolutionary act, let us do the same thing in here but for a different purpose. Let's, in our minds, roll back the tape of every single event that has ever taken place in this Universe. What we would see is called Singularity, the starting point for everything we pick with our five senses. From there, a colossal (but not infinite) number of events started to take shape. It is hard for me to imagine, and accept, that at some stage post-Big-Bang, these events started to become independent from each other. It is just like believing that in a flowing river, the water at a spot 50 meters downstream is not connected to the water at a point 50 meters upstream.

The water molecules in these two, and in every other spot of the river *are* connected, and those connections are called hydrogen bonds (2). The world's Events are also interconnected but in this case, the bonds are called "Information". About this, we shall have more, later.

One reason that might push us towards the belief that the world events are not uninterruptedly connected (a model which I would like to call the *"Fragmentary Model"*) is the gigantic size of the frame of reference, which in this case is the whole Universe. We could, quite understandably, ask ourselves, how could everything be related to everything else in a world with such astronomical dimensions? But let's not forget that all this super gigantic size, which is getting larger as we speak (3), originated from one tiny spot called Singularity. Once we realized that, it might be easier to convince ourselves that the very occurrence of the Bang set in motion the flow of every single event that has been happening ever since. To help clearly see what I mean, let me take you to the following thought experiment:

Let's close our eyes (just the physical ones not those of our minds) and imagine a laboratory in which you could initiate a Small Bang, a laboratory-scale model of the Big Bang. You do this by pumping energy in the form of a pulse from a super powerful LASER source into a super-high-vacuum reaction vessel in the form of a tunnel a few meters long. Every event that occurs in this tunnel would be visible to you, the Experimenter. The commencement of the bang ignites a chain of events that would not stop until a red button at the end of the tunnel is pushed in. When depressed, the red button sends a signal to another LASER source located in the ceiling of the tunnel, which in turn, shoots out a hail of evaporating photons. The evaporating photons then inject such a high dose of kinetic energy into anything in its path that "evaporates" them into their initial "creator light", or in other words, into a "material annihilation".

The "Events" begin with the formation of very simple particles which get more and more complicated in structure as the time goes on. The Events also take place absolutely independent of the surroundings, that is, the tunnel walls and the rest of the physical experimental set-up. They take place only in an "Events Bubble" which is nothing more than the segment of space in which all events of the Bang take place, a frame of reference. The Bubble is also wirelessly connected to a computerized detector that senses the occurrence of every single Event as well as its relationship to others. The totality of the Events makes the Bubble's environmental conditions. The Bubble's environmental conditions at any given instance are a result of each previous event and develop as the experiment progresses. The operating computer is programmed to display each event as a dot on the monitor in a perspective fashion, with the Small Bang itself as a central dot. Each new dot would be connected to any other dot that played a role in the formation of the new ones but any dot that has no effect on a following event would be deleted. A list of these deleted dots would be displayed in a column to the left side of the monitor screen. This would be the *"Deleted"* column. The overall picture of the connected dots would be a perspective (or 3-D-looking) figure of a sphere at the end of the experiment. The computer generates these graphics through the following procedure: It saves in its memory, a complete set of information on every single Event that occurs in the Bubble. For example, if there is a collision between two particles (described below), this set of information would include the energy of collision, the nature of particles involved, the pre- and post-collision coordinates of the particles in the Bubble, the coordinates of the collision itself, the post-collision remnant energies (if any), the nature of the product particles (if any), the direction of the movement of all particles after the collision. The computer then correlates each set of information with those acquired from the previous ones. These data acquisition/processing functions of the computer would generate a *virtual* "Information Sphere" which is simultaneously used to build the graphic representation.

After an extremely short period of time from the start of the bang, during which you had no idea as to what kind of events might have taken place, you notice the formation of a number of tiny particles. The particles were produced as a direct result of the nature and properties inherent in the LASER beam you used to initiate the Small Bang. As the time goes on, you see that some of the initial tiny particles would start coming together to make even larger and structurally more complicated ones. This combination process is a function of one factor and one factor only: The properties of each combining particle and those of the ones that surround them, if any. These properties are built-in, unalterable, and inherent. Some initial particles, however, stay as they were, depending on the availability of others to combine with and the level of their energy. Regardless of their type and nature, though, all may become not only the starting material for the next generation, but also the very "environment" and "condition" for future Events, playing a role in the development of the nature of anything and everything that would come later.

The experiment keeps going on, eventfully but smoothly, and the particles keep getting more and more complex. One thing is certain though: Combining or not, there is a constant and absolutely non-stop interaction of every single particle with others. That is why the computer-generated graphics on the monitor shows that every single dot is connected to the others, either directly (a first-order connection) or through other particles (a higher-order connection). This is a clear indication that in the Events Bubble, nothing is "born" independently and without a cause.

Some of the increasingly larger Things ("Things" because they are now too large and too complex to be called particles) have started showing a "branching" pattern within their own "particulate bodies" as well as a strange behavior: They are moving around using their own parts. They even move towards some other Things, absorb them, and make them parts of their own. Another observation that you made is the varieties in the ways these Things behave. Something similar was also noticed at the beginning of the experiment: A groups of particles, though only minutely different in their structure, behaved differently. And the difference in their behavior got more and more significant as they got more and more different in structure. But interestingly, all members of the same group, those with identical structures, did everything in exactly the same way. With Things, the same pattern is expressed although the number of the group members with the same behavior gets smaller as the degree of their complexity increases. Furthermore, the behavior of all Things was a definite and direct consequence of the initial particles forming them as well as the sequence of their coming together. For example, if we used numbers to tag each different group of particles, we will have P1, P2, P3, ..., Pn. When these particles combine to form Things, those made with the sequence [P1P2P3, ..., Pn] would behave differently than those with the [P2P3P1, ..., Pn] sequence.

The experiment continues rolling until one of the Things, now so well-combined and advanced that could detect the infrared (IR) light coming from the red-colored *"End"* button. You are so impressed with this little thing that you decide to give it a name, and its being IR-sensitive makes the naming easy: You call it "Crimson". Although all other Things in the same neighborhood are hit with that IR, there is something about Crimson that makes it susceptible to this wavelength. Upon a speedy review of the Small Bang's mechanism, you see no other reason for the IR-detecting ability of Crimson than the properties and combination sequences of its constituting particles. And there is more about Crimson that could make you proud of it: Right upon its IR detection, it dashes towards the red button at such a speed that the force of impact pushes the button in and terminates the experiment.

So, regardless of how far you intended to take it, your experiment is stopped and all that is left from it are your own observations recorded in your memory cells and the 3-D picture that the computer is showing you on its monitor. The screen shows the perspective image of thousands of tiny dots arranged in the shape of a sphere, with each dot connected to others by one or more straight lines. One of the dots sits exactly in the center of the sphere. This reminds you of a 3-D picture of a basketball with tiny millets filling its entire inner space and outer surface, with each grain of millet being tied to one or more of others by tightly stretched sewing threads. There are so many threads coming out of the central dot and its neighboring millets that it is hardly visible. But you know it is there because the whole ensemble is founded on it.

Despite its very complicated appearance, the picture on the monitor screen is not too hard to interpret: Formation of every single particle or Thing (including Crimson) is connected to at least one previous, and at least one next particle or Thing. And as for the interactions, even if a given dot is connected to just one dot, the latter one could be connected to several, and those "several" to other "several" and so forth, and as such, the overall pattern would be that of a very tightly knit spider web pattern, with the central point being the beginning Event. One other point of note is your observation that the *"Deleted"* column to the left of the screen is completely empty. This further confirms that no Event was detected which did not play a role in the development of future Events.

So What?

The Small Bang thought experiment draws an imaginary picture, of course. But imagination, especially when it could be extrapolated to the real world, may serve as a guiding light to show the way to a nonimaginary conclusion. This may not be a very pleasant analogy but it may be a fit one: Solely based on the victim's or a witness's memory and descriptions, a forensic artist may paint a picture of a criminal that would lead to an arrest. The Small Bang thought experiment attempts in drawing a simplified picture of Events' connectivity during and after what we now know as the Big Bang. Just like in this experiment, there is no reason that the original singularity state of the Big One could not be extended to the present and then into the future. In other words, that "Spider Web" pattern revealed at the end of the Small Bang experiment might be a valid model for the connectedness and the cause-and-effect mechanism of the universal Events. What could be the reason for not believing in a model of the world in which every Event is connected to the ones in its past and to those in its future by *"Threads of Information"*? From whatever knowledge available as of today, I cannot help but believe in some kind of "Information" which had been encrypted in the very essence of the Big Bang's energy at the singularity stage. The Info could have propagated outward from within the Singularity, not only to *determine* but to *become* the nature of every single event that occurred afterwards. And to clarify what I mean by "nature of events" let me use an example (this example focuses on only a tiny time point in the 13.7 billion years of the Universe's history but may be generalized to all points of that time window): An atom of the element sodium was produced by some type of thermonuclear reaction (TNR) in the core of a star (4). The information transferred from the parent atoms (those that were converted to sodium in the TNR) to sodium determined an arrangement of electrons around the nuclei which was *uniquely* specific to sodium. This arrangement makes the resulting atom nothing but sodium. In fact, it may be considered analogous to the transfer of genetic information from parent to offspring in the *Animalia* and *Plantae* kingdoms. Encrypted in the certain arrangement of sodium electrons is a message (a piece of information) that encodes, for example, for the violent reaction of sodium with water. In other words, the violent reactivity with water is a *nature* of sodium. Therefore, the information or message that was "inherited" by sodium from its parent atoms also becomes its nature. By the same token, applying this information mechanism to the Small Bang's Spider Web model, we could readily see that the connecting arms of the web would be, in fact, nothing but "Information" that connects any and all dots (or Events) together. Now here comes that question again: Why could this model not be applied to the Big Bang? I believe the answer is "it could", and the reason is what I would call the *"Energy-Information Duality, EID"* principle, the mutual encryption of energy and information: *Energy is information and information is energy.* Consider this: What is the nature of an electronic message such as a phone (SMS) text or an email? It's electromagnetic radiation (EMR) flying out of your device to the other side. What's EMR? It's pure energy in the form of photons. Your friend's device picks up those photons and translates them into words. Is it not logical to conclude that the EMR photons contained your message (which was really some type of information) within themselves, in the form of frequencies and wave lengths, which were all *uniquely* specific to every word, and the overall format, of your message? After all, it was those photons of energy, and nothing else, that carried that information over to your friend.

If the initial energy of the Bang has been able to so powerfully "fuel" the formation and operation of our Universe, and by "Universe" I mean *all* matter plus *all* Events, for the past 13.7 billion years, it must have also been able to transfer its Information, particle to particle, Thing to Thing, and therefore, Event to Event. This transfer of information could not have occurred had it not been for the fact that some initial message was originally encrypted in the Bang's energy. And that could mean only one thing: Energy is also information and information is also energy, or the EID phenomenon.

Having drawn that conclusion, however, I should bring up the possibility of a second phenomenon as follows. Should such a phenomenon as the EID have been a possibility, we would also be faced with two different scenarios:

Scenario 1. The totality of the operational information (also may also be called *"Instructions"* in this case) of the Universe, as to what was supposed to happen from the very beginning to the end, was encrypted in the original "package" of the Big Bang energy, and

Scenario 2. The development of each Event leads to an *in situ* generation of the Information for the Events that followed. An example of this scenario could be, again, the formation of the sodium atom. Once the atom was made (we ignore the causes leading to its making for the time being), the information related to its properties was formed and carried on with it.

As I mentioned before in Chapter 10, the method employed to arrive at the conclusion of this book is proving, by relying on scientific givens, that Causal Determinism is the operational mechanism of our world. Accordingly, from the two scenarios defined above, the first one has to be ruled out as it is not compatible with the definition and meaning of Causal Determinism. In fact, Scenario 1 clearly represents Predeterminism and Fatalism doctrines better than it does Causal Determinism. The two former doctrines are not what I believe should hold, and therefore, Scenario 1 is to be abandoned. Scenario 2, however, seems to be exactly what you would expect from a causally determined universe that functions according to a cause-and-effect mechanism.

Now there may be a barrier (and practically a sizable one) sitting in the way of the vessel of our logic to the destination of "acceptance", the acceptance of what has been discussed in the last few paragraphs. That barrier is the size and dimensions of our Universe as compared to those of any thought experiment. Even if performing of the Small Bang thought experiment would have been possible, and even if it were carried out in a tunnel as lengthy as that of the

CERN's (*Conseil Européen pour la Recherche Nucléaire*; French: *European Organization for Nuclear Research*) Large Hadron Collider in Geneva, Switzerland, a 27-kilometers-long tunnel, could we generalize the outcomes to something as gigantic as our Universe? The relative size of a 27-kilometers-long anything, compared to the known diameter of even the Milky Way galaxy would be close to zero let alone compared to that of the whole Universe.[1] But let's see if we could get passed that barrier:

We humans and our measuring scales are infinitesimally small relative to the size of the Cosmos. Therefore, it would not be unexpected if we looked at the world through our tiny measuring scales and ask that barrier question: "How the immeasurably *large* number of Events that have occurred during such a *long* period of time, and within such a *large* space, can all be interrelated not only with each other but with the very beginning point of singularity?"

The concepts of "size", "dimension", and "quantity", are all relative. Compared to a star located 4 million light years from Earth, a star at 2 light years may be considered just next door. The Universe *is* immensely large but only according to *our* measuring scales. Just for the sake of argument, imagine the size of our planet Earth and everything in it, including us, suddenly grew by a factor of one billion times while dimensions of everything else in the world stayed the same. It would not be too hard to picture that, under that condition, everything else could have looked one billion times smaller. Additionally, while this is a (relatively) huge Universe which has been expanding at an accelerated rate, it is the very same smaller one as it was, say, one million years after the Big Bang, with its energy-information package. So, if we accept that the Universe started out with the EID principle in its essence, we should also accept that it works according to a "Spider Web Information Transfer" model, and therefore, through a "Cause-and-Effect" mechanism.

The Product

So, after all that has been discussed so far, what would be the take-home conclusion of this book, or as we may call it, the final product of our synthesis? By now, I am sure you have at least an abstract idea about it but let's try to put everything in a final order, as "order" enhances our abilities for better understanding, analyzing, evaluating, and decision making about any issue.

We started out from the Big Bang theory (BBT), the theory of the birth of our Universe. Naturally, as everything that followed was based on this one theory, its validity should have been of fundamental importance. Fortunately, the BBT enjoys solid support through more than one scientific evidence which were listed in Chapter 2. The Causal Deterministic theory (or the No-Choice theory in this book) has its base in the BBT by proposing that:

1. All post-BB Events are parts of a *single* and *continuous* flow of interconnected information-transfer processes which will run into the future and through the lifetime of our Universe.
2. The single *"glue"* that sustains universal Events' interconnectivity is the phenomenon of *"Causality"*.
3. Causality is the *essential* driving force for the occurrence of any and all Events and is the reflection of the information acquired from an immediate previous Event onto a future Event.
4. Causality also initiated the formation of matter as the reflection of the transferred information encrypted in the Singularity energy.
5. The nature of atoms comprising Matter is dictated by their nuclear and electronic configurations which themselves are the reflections of their Causality.
6. The nature and number of particles comprising Matter are, at the same time, both an Effect of the last, and the Cause for the next, Event.

7. The nature and number of particles comprising Matter along with their spatial coordinates form the *Environment* which is, in part, the Cause for future Events.
8. The nature and number of particles comprising Matter also determine the mechanism of *Energy Exchange Processes (EEP's)*.
9. EEP's are responsible for intersystem exchanges of information due to the principle of *Energy-Information Duality (EID)*.
10. The *Resultant Overall Effects* of propositions 1-9 have led to a *Deterministic* Universe.

The preceding propositions suggest that the path of evolution of the Universe was determined according to the essential information of the original energy of the Big Bang. The propagation and transfer of this EID, however, took place according to Scenario 2 discussed earlier in this chapter. It was this information, or code, that led to the formation of particulate matter. From there, everything proceeded according to the properties of every single particle of matter and their interactions within infinitesimally small, but continuous, segments of time. This chain reaction gradually led to the formation of increasingly more complicated systems, each undergoing a Cause-and-Effect process. The elements of the Periodic Table were formed one by one with each one determined only by the properties of its parent particles and the EID of its Environment. Even the energetic aspects of their synthesis and the corresponding environmental conditions, were results of the surrounding matter (4). As such, elements (atoms), each with specific chemical properties and specific locations (coordinates), came to existence in the universal space. Both the chemical properties and the spatial coordinates of each generation of particles were determined by those of their parent atoms and the produced particles themselves determined those of the coming generations. The continuous interactions of particles formed more and more complicated and larger ones that now we know as molecules. Just like the simpler and smaller beginning atoms, the properties of these molecules have been a direct result of their specific structures. The way the constituting atoms have come together and have been arranged in a molecule determines the chemical, physical, and mechanical properties of that molecule. And again, the nature and spatial coordinates of those "constituting atoms" are the only factors that determine what kind of product molecules would be made. All the information that is needed to guide a process to the next step is coded within all components of this Universe, be it matter or energy.

As for the larger combinations of the more advanced molecules, those classified as the *Animalia* and *Plantae* kingdoms, they are also the exact functions of their structures. They are machines in which movements of their parts are determined by how the atoms and molecules of their genetic systems had been bonded together. The codes encrypted in their genome determine the structures of their whole system. In animals, their whole system also includes their brains that command and control all their mental and physical activities: How to move, how to eat, how to grow, how to react and respond to the stimuli from their environment which includes other large combinations of atoms and molecules that do the same things. And the nature and pattern of arrangement of the atoms and molecules that shape brains, also tell the "holders" of those brains how to think. That is, how they think is determined by their structures and those structures are nothing but the *kind*, *number*, and *arrangement* of their atoms. In plants, although brain as a defined structure does not exist, living mechanisms are based on the same structure-function principles (refer, for example, to the working mechanism of plant tendrils discussed in chapter 8).

In addition to the individual structural factors and variables, the "fate" of Things ("Thing" with capitalized "T" refers to *any* form of matter, from atoms to humans) is determined by their interactions with their environment also. The Environment affects Things according to its own properties which arise from its own contents due to the action-reaction principle. In the case of animals and plants, the information from any environmental effect is processed in their brains, or any organ that is developed to process information. In other words, whatever changes that is made as a result of interactions between any entities and their surroundings, is determined by the type, properties, number, and arrangements of the atoms involved from all interacting participants. And since the "atoms involved" and their arrangements are "fixed" entities (that is, have a given structure at any given point in time), those changes are causatively determined.

So, there it is, our deterministic picture: The Big Bang's initial energy, containing the initiating information (instructions) brought about another form of energy that we call Matter (recall $E = mc^2$, Chapter 4), then Matter behaved according to the instructions encoded in it (recall the sodium atom example). Within the course of this *"chain reaction"*, matter also generated energy (*e.g.*, star-core gravity-generated heat) that created other forms of matter in the form of chemical elements which eventually led to the development of Things we call plants and animals. Every newly formed Thing, from atoms to molecules, to rocks, birds, trees, us, *etc.*, was developed according to the instructions (information) contained in the atoms of both, its immediate "predecessors" (or parents) and in those of the Environment they were formed within. No Thing has been, is, or will be, independent of other Things and it is this *collective* and *structure/information-based* interaction among Things that determines Events and make the world deterministic, or in other words, *fixed structure creates fixed fate*. I should emphasize that, in the context of this discussion, "Structure" refers to the structures of *all* components of the Universe, taken into account simultaneously and within each given section of time. The degrees of interaction among these components to lead to any Event, however, varies and is determined by their spatial coordinates. In the development of causally determined Events, no structure is to be considered completely isolated from others.

Based on what I have shared with you so far, it is my belief that the functioning model of our world is an *"Interactive Spider Web"* model, and no matter how much this Universe has grown, or will grow in both size and complexity, the overall interconnections and interactions among its constituting elements have been and will be a continuous-flow phenomenon which we may justly call "Causality". And as long as a system, such as the Cosmos, works through the causality mechanism, that system is deterministic. And in our deterministic world there can be no choices and no "custom-made" selections which could be made according to our Freewill. Freewill is an illusion, created because we only *think* we make our choices freely. In the case of us humans, our *Homo sapiens* pride keeps our mind in the Freewill box which, by the way, has thick and sometimes impermeable, walls. In reality, though, our decisions, choices, and selections are made according to two variables: Our individual structures and those of the components of the rest of the world, that is, our "Environment". Events that shape this world are strictly structure-based and Things have no choice but to follow the functional outcomes of those structures. The cell phone that you are using probably every day, even if it's a "smart" one, cannot fly (at least not just yet) because it's not designed to fly. It does *only* what it's been designed to do and it does *only* what its structure is capable of doing. The same is true of everything else in this world including our bodies and our brains. Our brains make our choices and decisions according to their structure and the very fine details of those structures, and those structures have their roots in events and processes dating back billions of years ago. We may think of our minds, psyches, and spirits as entities with supernatural powers and abilities but, at the end of the day, all of those powers and abilities originate from, and are created in, a material 3-D structure called Central Nervous System and according to their interactions with another material and 3-D structure called the Environment, which by the way is both internal *and* external. It would be only a very short-sighted view to isolate our brains, and every Thing else in the world, from other Things, Events, and processes, that like the protein chains of a spider web, have been interconnected from the very beginning of creation up to the moment of our making a decision.[2] It may not be the most pleasant of conclusions but we, just like that cell phone, are functions of our structures, which themselves are the results of their predecessors' designs, and those "designs" were surely the will-less resultants of the number, the nature, and the arrangement of their parent atoms and those of their environments, all the way back to the Bang. There is no isolated, independent, self-controlled, and therefore, freewill being anywhere in this Universe. If there is a Thing, it *has* to be at least informationally connected to other Things and every ensuing Event would be the result of those connections. Like it or not, we, and "we" in this case means everything and everyone that our five senses could detect, are *all* connected, both existentially and functionally, to one another and to the very Origin of our Universe. Everything and everyone is the "Effect" of its previous "Cause" and Determinism is the rule of the game.

What About Chaos?

If some of the events in Nature are chaotic, then how could the world be deterministic? I tried to answer this question in Chapter 11 but due to the importance of this theory as applied to Determinism, a short reminder here may be in order. The difficulty that I have with the way that Chaos Theory is perceived in relation to Determinism is that the theory has been interpreted as a support for Indeterminism. The argument from those who ask that question is that the Universe is a dynamical system, the behavior of dynamical systems at any time in the future is ultrasensitive to changes in their initial conditions; measurement of the initial conditions of dynamical systems with 100% accuracy is not possible, therefore *prediction* of their behavior at any future time is impossible, and thus, the Universe cannot be a Deterministic system. To me (and I am sure to some others), there is a "misconnection" in this argument. The misconnection is attaching our lack of ability to correctly predict future Events to the deterministic or nondeterministic nature of the world. As discussed in Chapter 11, what happens in any dynamical process is independent of our ability to predict it. The reason for this, in my opinion, is that at each given moment (or any segment of time during which an Event commences) there can be no other Events which may have the exact same properties. Those properties are spacetime (*1*) coordinates (the location and coordinate time of the Event with the Big Bang as time zero) and the energy-related properties. The latter property includes any characteristics related to momentum and physical structures at any level. Any other Event, no matter how similar, is a different Event. This is equal to saying that, in each point in time, one and only one Event could take place and none other. If we couple this conclusion to the universal interconnectedness of Events based on the Spider Web Model, we should be able to also conclude that even chaotic Events follow a deterministic mechanism of development. For some additional related discussion, also, refer to the *Walking Droplet Experiment* in the next section.

WHAT ABOUT QUANTUM PHYSICS?

This is the Big One! At least from one angle of view, the highest hurdle in the way to argue for Determinism are the teachings of quantum physics, the seemingly ultimate "Probabilistic" doctrine.

As discussed in Chapter 12, the most frequently cited interpretation of quantum physics is the Copenhagen interpretation (Chapter 12 and reference 17 therein) which suggests that events (representing the behavior of physical systems) are but a collection of possibilities, each represented by a wave function.[3] Once an act of measurement (or observation) is attempted, only *one* possibility manifests itself as the *"Reality"*, in a hypothetical process referred to as "wave function collapse". The Copenhagen Interpretation (CI) implies that prediction of exactly what becomes Reality is not possible because we could not know which one of those possibilities becomes Reality, or in other words, which one of those wave functions would collapse to Reality. As disappointing as this conclusion was, most scientists (excluding Einstein and some others though) decided to accept it and be content with only the ability to calculate the probabilities and not the exact Realities. Interestingly, Erwin Schrödinger, the scientist who originally developed the concept of and the equation for wave functions, and the creator of Schroc, was himself among the people who opposed the CI (5).

We have already discussed these aspects of quantum physics in the last chapter, but as I said at the end of that chapter, there are other views of this seemingly strange science, which may be more leaning towards Determinism. One of these is called the *"Pilot-Wave Theory"*. Pilot Wave Theory was proposed by Louise de Broglie in the early 1920's but was abandoned in 1927 mainly due to the wide reception of the CI. With Einstein's encouragement, the renowned American theoretical physicist David Bohm (1917-1992) revisited the theory in 1952, made some modifications, and proposed the package as the *"de Broglie-Bohm theory"*, a.k.a., *"Bohm's Interpretation"*, *"Causal Interpretation"*, or the *"Pilot-Wave Theory"* (6). Unlike the CI, the de Broglie-Bohm theory is capable of dealing with the dynamics of a system with no intervention from an observer. That is, you don't need to look at something for the Reality to materialize.

Discussing and showing the very difficult and highly specialized mathematical details of this theory is way beyond the scope of this book, but the reason that I am citing the Pilot-Wave Theory (PWT) is that unlike the CI, PWT demonstrates a deterministic interpretation of quantum mechanics. Just like the classical Newtonian deterministic view of Nature, PWT suggests that the future evolves from the past, and therefore, if the physical states of all particles in the Universe are precisely known at any given time, their states at any future time may be calculated (remember that from the point of view of the Chaos theory "precisely known" may be a limiting factor, but theoretically, this statement is true). This is exactly what the classical Newtonian mechanics does for the macroscopic world. In fact, groups of scientists who were able to think out of the box, have been performing revolutionary experiments to prove the validity of the PWT. The first of these, the so-called *"Walking Droplet Experiment"* was reported by Yves Couder at Paris Diderot University in Paris, France (*7, 8, 9*). In these experiments, a tiny droplet of silicon oil is placed on the surface of the same kind of oil in a vibrating pan. Vibrations are adjusted to be weak enough so they do not produce any waves on the oil surface but strong enough to keep the droplet moving on the surface with a thin layer of air in between. This system is set to mimic the behavior of particles at quantum scales. It has been reproducibly observed that, rather than an indefinite pattern (which might have been predicted by the CI), the movement of the droplets on the oil surface is driven, and determined, by what the researchers call "path memory". Every bounce of the floating droplet creates ripples as path memories on the oil surface that *"chaotically but deterministically"* affect the droplets' future bounces. Importantly, the overall patterns of these bounces and movements have been shown to obey quantum-like statistics. As John Bush, a Professor of Applied Mathematics at MIT put it in a comment about these experiments "as the particles [droplets] move along, they feel the wave field generated by them in the past and all other particles in the past" (*10*). By this statement, Dr. Bush points to the deterministic nature of the path of the droplets as each one is guided by a pilot wave generated in their past, a case of cause-and-effect phenomenon.

If these experiments are true models of the quantum world, and the quantum world provides a true model of the macroscopic Universe, then they have been able to show the deterministic universal connectedness of particles and Things that we talked about earlier. Even from a quantum-physical point of view, the de Broglie-Bohm theory and its Pilot-Wave model suggest that there is a single (rather than many as suggested by the CI) wave function that governs all of the particles in the Universe and the movement of one particle depends on the position of all of the other particles, a phenomenon not unlike what we discussed in the Small Bang experiment earlier in this chapter. Every Event is the Effect of a previous Cause, and as such, the world works by a deterministic mechanism.

Now, while keeping the above discussions in mind, let me offer my personal view about quantum theory and Determinism: The quantum theory was put together (or maybe we could even say "discovered") by some genius observations and through studies of the elements of the micro-universe such as photons and electrons. As of now, the mainstream quantum physicists support the Copenhagen Interpretation (CI) of the theory, which as we learned earlier which proposes a probabilistic Universe and rejects Determinism. An example is Schroc the cat in the Schrödinger Cat paradox (Chapter 12). According to the CI, Schroc could be both dead *and* alive, in the sealed chamber and out of view, until somebody (or some Thing such as a detector) "observes" the result. Only at that time would Schroc's faith be a Reality.

Personally, I have a good bit of trouble accepting this proposition. To me, Events happen regardless of our observing them. At the same time, the quantum theory is built on solid grounds and is not something one could simply reject or ignore. On the other hand, and as I mentioned above, quantum theory was developed by observations and calculations at microscales. And in that world, the particles that were used (photons, electrons, protons, *etc.*) were absolutely identical and behaving in unison. So, after some thinking to see how I could come to an all-compromising hypothesis, I now believe quantum behavior is limited to particles, either microscopic *or* macroscopic, that are 100% identical. Since in the whole of the macro-world, being 100% identical is an impossible condition to be met by all of its components (or Things), the CI is inapplicable, and therefore irrelevant, and as such, would not be capable of rejecting Determinism. Now one might argue that if that's the case, how do you justify, for example, the radioactive decay process? As a refresher, recall that every radioactive element has its own half-life (shown as $t_{1/2}$) as described in Chapter 12, which is the time taken for any collection of radioactive atoms to decay to half of their original mass. In this process the atoms decay to produce their "daughter element(s)" and there is no way to tell exactly which atoms within that collection are to be decayed. This may be viewed as the embodiment of an absolutely random process. By my proposition, since in any given sample of any element, each and every one of those atoms is physically, energetically, and therefore *informationally*, 100% identical to each and every other atom, and all of them have well-defined and identical symmetries, we should be allowed to think of the whole ensemble as one single unit, as if we had one large atom with a definite mass. That single unit now has the property of losing half of its mass to radioactive decay. This not only removes the randomness factor, but also introduces an element of determinism into the process. The reason goes back to what we discussed earlier in this Chapter, in section *"So What?"* Based on what was discussed there, we may view an ensemble of any radioactive atoms as one single atom which is the product (or Effect) of earlier Causes (parent atoms and environmental conditions) with its built-in program as its physical and chemical properties, including its radioactive decay reaction with an element-specific $t_{1/2}$. And as such, we would be dealing with a deterministic system even in radioactive elements.

So, the way I look at such quantum theory interpretations as the CI and their implied rejection of Determinism, is that there has to be 100% homogeneity in size and shape (for which I invented the words "microscopicity" and "identicality", respectively), for a collection of particles (or Things) to exist in a quantum state. In other words, in a collection of Things, all particles have to be microscopic and 100% identical to one another before the ensemble could to be a "fit" for Copenhagen interpretation. And as such, macroscopic systems, which include us and the world we live in, could not be interpreted through the CI.

Now let's visit the Double-Slit (D-S) experiments described in Chapter 12 one more time. According to the CI, these experiments are outstanding examples of the collapse of wave functions and represent the probabilistic nature of the world (although the de Broglie-Bohm theory, and the recent Walking Droplet experiments claim that the D-S experiments are deterministic). To refresh your memory, groups of particles such as photons and electrons, were shot through two narrow slits in one screen and hit a second screen that registered the collisions. It was observed that particles produced a diffraction pattern, meaning they behaved like waves. Then they were shot through the same system, except this time one by one, to see if the wave-like behavior could be changed to particle behavior. It did not. Singly shot particles still behaved like waves. Then they installed detectors at the slits at which time particles behaved like particles. This was taken as the proof that, when looked at, only one possibility was the Reality but otherwise the particles showed all possibilities without revealing how. A bunch of theories, even philosophical ones, came out of the D-S experiments but it was also taken as a solid proof for the CI, and therefore, for the correctness of the wave function collapse hypothesis pointing to a probabilistic world, and thus, for the rejection of Determinism.

As of this writing, the D-S experiment has been carried out with photons, electrons, protons, and believe it or not, with buckyballs.[4] All of these particles meet both of the requirements of "microscopicity" and "identicality" (again, my invented words) and therefore they could meet the requirement of being quantum particles when they were put through the experiment. While nobody could deny the reproducibility of the results, I believe even if they behaved probabilistically and obeyed the CI, they did so because of their existence as quantum particles and at quantum scales, which may not be applicable to the macroscopic world. As such, the results of this type of experiments may not reject or exclude the possibility of Determinism as the working mechanism of our macro-world. In fact, this conclusion brings me to a new proposition: If the there are two different mechanisms that separately control the micro- and the macro-worlds, there may exist a margin that separates the quantum-ruling micro-world from our Deterministic macro-universe. I call such a hypothetical separating margin a *"Threshold Membrane"*.

Not unrelated to this subject and just as a side note, once I was watching a video on one of the talks of Thomas Campbell, a bright physicist and writer, about the D-S experiment. He mentioned how the D-S experiment has been performed with different particles like photons, electron, protons, and Bucky Balls, and how all gave the same result. And then to emphasize on the universality of the D-S experimental outcomes, he stated ".. in fact, you could throw a toaster oven at it [the slits] and it would work." With all due respect, I could not disagree more with that statement. A toaster oven, or anything of that nature, is neither microscopic nor is it composed of identical particles. Rather, it has sizable dimensions and is made with more than one type of particle. And plus, nobody has ever done a D-S experiment with any macroscopic object even smaller than a toaster oven. This is one of those cases that you really need to do the test before announcing the results.

In their book, *"The Great Design"* (11), the renowned theoretical physicist, Stephen Hawking and his co-author Leonard Mlodinow make the following remarks, which interestingly, relate to both our hypothetical Threshold Membrane and the Toaster Oven Throw:

> "...And though the component atoms obey the principles of quantum physics, one can show that the large assemblages that form soccer balls, turnips, and jumbo jets-and us- will indeed manage to avoid diffracting through slits. So though the components of everyday objects obey quantum physics, Newton's laws form an effective theory that describes very accurately how the composite structures that form our everyday world behave."

Notes

[1] The diameter of the Milky Way has been estimated to be around 100 light years. A light year is the *distance* travelled by light within one Earth year. This distance is equal to 9.4608×10^{12} (9,460.8 billion) kilometers or 5.913×10^{12} (5,913 billion) miles.

[2] Spider webs are proteins. Like all proteins they are chains of amino acids linked together through peptide bonds (discussed in Chapter 5). The web protein is secreted from spinneret glands located at the tip of the spiders' abdomen.

[3] "Physical systems" refers to anything that could affect, and be detected by, one or more of our five senses. Naturally, that would be the material world that surrounds us.

[4] Buckyballs are ball-shaped large molecules made exclusively of carbon atoms which belong to the fullerene family of organic compounds. Their full name is buckminsterfullerene, after the American architect Richard Buckminster Fuller (1895-1983), as a tribute to his famous geodesic dome designs.

REFERENCES

1. Ashby N, Relativity in the Global Positioning System, *Liv Rev Rel*, 6: 16, 2003. DOI: 10.12942/lrr-2003-1
2. Arunan E, *et al.*, Definition of the Hydrogen Bond, *Pure Appl Chem*, 83 (8): 1637–1641, 2011. DOI: 10.1351/PAC-REC-10-01-02
3. Radford T, Universe is Expanding up to 9% Faster than We Thought, Say Scientists, *The Guardian*, 3 June, 2016.
4. Shultis JK and Faw RE, *Fundamentals of Nuclear Science and Engineering*, CRC Press, p. 151, ISBN 0-8247-0834-2.
5. Schrödinger E, Die gegenwärtige Situation in der Quantenmechanik (German: "The Present Situation in Quantum Mechanics"), *Naturwissenschaften*, 23 (48): 807–812, 1935. DOI: 10.1007/BF01491891
6. Bohm D, A Suggested Interpretation of the Quantum Theory in Terms of "Hidden Variables" I&II, *Phys Rev*, 85 (2): 166–179, 1952. DOI: 10.1103/PhysRev.85.166
7. Couder Y, Proti`ere S, Fort E, Boudaoud A, Walking and Orbiting Droplets, *Nature*, 437: 208, 2005.
8. Proti`ere S, Boudaoud A, Couder Y, Particle Wave Association on Fluid Interface, *J Flu Mech*, 554: 85-105, 2006.
9. Wolchover N, In: *Wired*, 30 June, 2014. URL: https://www.wired.com/2014/06/the-new-quantum-reality/
10. Bush, JWM, Pilot-Wave Hydrodynamics, *Ann Rev Fl Mech*, 49: 269-292, 2014.
11. Hawking S, Mlodinow L, *The great Design*, Bantam Books, New York, 2010, ISBN: 978-0-553-80537-6, Chapter 4, p. 67.

CHAPTER 14

Translation

—∞—

"Reason is the ultimate justification for knowledge."

RENÉ DESCARTES

IN THE PREVIOUS CHAPTERS WE talked about the possible existence of a universal informational interconnection between energy and matter. The rationale for this proposition was based on the scientifically supported partial conversion of energy to matter during the Big Bang. This, I argued, must have been in parallel to a simultaneous transfer of information from energy to matter. This information transfer then resulted in the development of different structural features in matter, and from there, in specific properties of different types of matter. While, from a physical transformation point of view, these processes may be viewed as well-differentiated stages, fundamentally they are only another form of an energy-matter conversion process according to the $E = mc^2$ equation (see Chapter 4). The information transfer aspect was a byproduct of these conversions which occurred due to the "Energy-Information Duality" principle, discussed in the last chapter. If such a duality existed, it would be logical to consider that it was not dissociable, meaning, when there is energy, there is information and *vice versa*. On the other hand, although conversions of one form of energy to another one of its different forms, including matter, may be taken as discrete processes, since the properties of each newly formed particle of matter is determined by the information inherited from its parent particles, the flow of information has to be a continuous process. As such, it should be logical to also consider that all particles of matter and all packets (quanta) of energy have been informationally interconnected from the beginning of time.

Every structure, micro- or macroscopic, is the product of a series of stepwise processes. These processes were initiated and then progressed according to the information encrypted in the initial energy of the Big Bang and in those energies and material particles produced thereafter. Based on the principle of Structure-Function Relationship (Chapter 8), the properties, nature, and thus, behavior of any entity depends on the design of its structure, which in turn, has been produced according to the rules of Causal Determinism. The variety in the nature, properties, and behavior of any entity is directly proportional to the extent of its complexity. For example, there is almost no difference between the properties of two identical atoms or molecules under the same ambient conditions. But when the very same atoms or molecules combine with billions of others to make horses, the characteristics of any two horses may not be the same. In the case of humans, the degree of their behavioral variations may be the highest among all other organisms due to the complexity of their brains structures. The properties of our brains complex structures, all the way down to their molecular make-up, *in part*, form our personalities, characters, and overall psyches. The reason I say "in part" is twofold: First, in addition to the structure of our brains itself, the structure of the rest of our body is also important as it determines our mechanical and physiological characteristics, factors which in their own right, play determining roles in the determination of our personalities and psychology. Second, we are also products of our environment, not only physically but also psychologically. And by "Environment" I mean more than the weather and geographical location of the place we live in. In this discussion, Environment means everything and anything outside our physical and mental "selves". Within a broad spectrum, it means other human beings, plants, animals, cars, buildings, *etc.*, and yes, the weather and the geological locations. So, who we are, what we do, and how we behave is determined by two factors, *Genome* and *Ecology*, themselves shaped by a combination of Cause-and-Effect mechanisms.

Taking all that was just said into account, we could be led to one important conclusion: If every particle of matter and every quantum of energy carries with it "bits" of information which we call "properties" of that particle or that packet of energy, then everything and everyone is, *at least informationally*, connected to everything and everyone else.[1,2] This interpretation of our Universe is, of course, nothing but the Universal Spider Web Interconnectivity (USWI) model which was described in the last chapter and may be used to explain the mechanism of a deterministic world.

Now we should think about how all these hypotheses translate into the reality of our lives as humans? The short Translation is that if the USWI model holds, every single past, present, and future Event has been, is being, and shall be determined according to the overall structure of the Universe at each given point in time. And since this Universe could have only one single and definite structure at each given point in time, it could produce only one single, definite, and thus determined, Event at each point in time. No imaginary "probabilities" and no "invisible possibilities". The series of Events that originated from the Big Bang and led to the formation of us and our brains, all have been deterministic processes. Our brain has a defined structure, which in combination with the environmental effectors (with the definition of Environment as given above), shape our decisions and behaviors. It should be noted here that the process of "Formation" (of anything) has been a 13.7-billion-year-old continuous and uninterrupted process. So, when I talk about the definite structure of our brains and that of the Environment, it should be kept in mind that these structures are part of an "Information Continuum", again considering that any property of anything is the same as the information encoded within that Thing. If we divide those 13.7 billion years into, for example, 1-second-long time sections, and each section contains so many Events, each single Event in each single 1-second section would be related and connected to the ones contained in the previous section as well as to those in the following section. That's what I mean by a "continuum" which allows for absolutely no isolated incidence.

Furthermore, the defined structure of our brains, as well as all the interacting environmental factors, are subject to change, of course, and those changes too affect our decisions and behaviors. But the factors that bring about those changes are also determined according to their own internal and environmental effectors. So, in reality we and everyone and everything else are only "programmed" within a deterministically produced body. Remember the example of Sodium in Chapter 13? Because of its electronic structure, sodium is programmed to (among other activities) react violently with water and as long as it retains that particular atomic structure, it would always react violently with water. And if it does not retain that particular structure, it would no longer be "sodium". In this same example, three factors come into play to determine the outcome of the interaction of sodium with water: Sodium's atomic structure, water's molecular structure, and sodium's surrounding environment, which, in this case, is only water. The same mechanism, only at a universal scale, determines our and everything else's life events: Atomic and molecular structures of both the "Subject" (*i.e.*, me, you, your fifth cousin's favorite oak tree, *etc.*) *and* those of each corresponding surrounding environment, interact in a simultaneous and synchronized manner and the overall outcome is Life in its absolute and Universal sense. And any consequential change in the structure of the components of the Universe would be an Effect which becomes a Cause for further Effects, and the Life flows along the arrow of Time in such a deterministic fashion. In short, you may think of the working of the World as to be the same as that of your watch: According to its structural design. That "You" in you who thinks, analyzes your life issues, makes decisions, loves, or hates, helps or hurts, is nothing but the product of your genetically inherited structure and that of your surrounding environment, evolved continuously and in a harmonious parallel with every Thing and every One else which has been in the making since the beginning of Time.

Now let's go back to a bit more specific and more human-related issue, the puzzle of "having" or "not having" Freewill. The belief in Freewill is so deeply ingrained in our minds that we should not be surprised to see those "rolling eyes" anytime we try to argue against it. It is analogous to a situation like when you try to convince someone, who has absolutely no previous knowledge about mirages, that what he sees is really not water on the ground. We see very clearly that we can do what we want to do and don't do what we don't, that is, under normal conditions, of course. The only reason we believe we possess Freewill is that we are aware of our decisions and our actions. But being aware of our decisions and actions is very different than having the absolute freedom in making them. You may ask: "So why, when I was offered five different desserts on the menu, I could pick exactly the one I liked the best? That's my Freewill." Sorry to disappoint you but it's not your Freewill. The wiring of your brains, which by the way was determined how to be billions of years ago, told you which one of those deserts you (or in reality, "It", the arrangement and wiring pattern of your brain cells) were supposed to like the best. Your brain then commanded your arm muscles to flex your fingers and grab that particular piece of cake, even under the watchful gaze of your Significant Other who was concerned about your cholesterol level. The whole process, or Event, was nothing but a programmed interaction of molecules among themselves and with their Environment that created the illusion of your making your selection through a Freewill.

Although I have talked about these before, I should remind you of, and emphasize on, a couple of point, here:

1. By "programmed" in this case I do not mean "pre-programmed" but a process that becomes an "actuality" according to the structure of your system. To clarify this, I am afraid, I have to make another unpleasant, even cruel, hypothetical situation (I sincerely hope it'll never happens to you): Suppose just before you were able to make a choice on that dessert, you came down with a heart attack and died. If they did an autopsy on your brain, nobody could find a "program" anywhere inside of your brains or your CNS that said "yep, the Key lime cheese cake". Rather, your selection of that dessert would have been the product of a number of interactions among your CNS cells (and also indirectly the rest of your body), which themselves were a product of that long 13.7-billion-year process we discussed earlier, and,
2. The word "Environment" means everything and everyone out of your physical and mental "Self". These, also remember, have been and are all interconnected through the Information bridges of the Universal Spider Web Interconnectivity network.

So, let's be humble enough, and logical enough, to accept the fact that what we do is only a harmonious act of structures and that we live and function as per our own, and our Environment's, designs. To me it's not a weakness to be in this way and to agree with that reality, it's just the way things work and we have absolutely no choice but to accept it. Weakness and strength are relative terms. Reality, on the other hand, is absolute. It is the one single way in which Events occur and become "actualities". The act of accepting the "Absolute" cannot be judged by "relative" scales and measures. To me personally, just being able to understand and accept the "Facts", and the way they are, is courageous enough. At the very least, it could show how high one has been able to ascend on the ladder of mind evolution to be able to break open the casts that our minds might have been imprisoned in for so long.

What About Moral Responsibility?

Some of the strongest oppositions to Determinism and lack of Freewill have been based on the issues of moral responsibility, and ethics. Arguments against a lack of Freewill, and thus against Determinism itself, from the points of view of moralities are plentiful. We may hear the opponents say, "If we have no Freewill and can act only according to the structure of our brains, then how are we supposed to deal with moral issues?", or "If we grant that humans have no power to make their decisions at will, would we not be issuing a free ticket to anarchy and destruction of humane values? How are we supposed to treat criminals?", and "If a murderer *was supposed* to kill, how we could punish him for his crime because the committer was deterministically set to commit that crime?" My answer is this: "How to answer those questions is *our* problem." Unfortunately, with all their ugliness and all the pains that they could cause, crimes are our problems not Nature's. Judicial laws by which we try the societies' wrong doers are manmade, and as such, have no accommodations within the laws of Nature. What we do, on the other hand, is a direct consequence of the law of Nature, and therefore, it should not come with surprise if no preventive measures against our personal and sociological problems and are foreseen in it.

Nature does not care if the loss of a dear friend makes me extremely sad. Nature works according to its structure and that structure includes and encompasses everything, including us, our actions, and our decisions. And no, that structure does not always guarantee a happy ending for all Events. Changing some of the outcomes of its structural features, because of some painful consequences that they may produce, is not included in its mechanisms. If it were, we would never see an innocent little gazelle, that feels fear and pain just as much as you and I do, running with its heart in its throat and then ripped apart alive just because a pack of lions was hungry. Lions are biological machines. They consume energy, and when they run out of it, their brains tell them to eat. And when they get the signal, they go to work. No lion ever thinks "Oh, I just can't bring myself to kill that innocent gazelle. How could I look into her mom's eyes next time I run into her on the plain?" Lions kill when hungry because their structures tell them to. Or maybe you want a human-related example. How about this one: If Nature were capable of feeling and understanding our problems, sufferings, and pains, why then somebody would be born with a silver spoon in his mouth, well-supported and never having to worry about hunting a job all his life, and another, just as human as the first one, is born into poverty, has to swallow his childhood dreams of nice toys and clothes, and just see them in his dreams (if he is not too hungry to fall asleep), and labors hard just to survive until he dies? Does Nature care? And although it cannot be generalized across the populations, but what are the possibilities of the first individual to become a wrong-doer as compared to the second one? As far as Nature is concerned, if the "conditions" of the coming to this world for those two fellows are the way that they were just described, so be it. Not Nature's problem. In fact, Nature does not, and cannot, feel the depths and the pains of any problems simply because it is not capable of having a compassion, period. Nature just works according to the instructions that are encrypted in it. We could have had the right to ask those questions, should every human being have been born and raised in exactly the same condition and with access to exactly the same privileges (although I still believe we couldn't, but just for the sake of the argument). But it's not like that. Way too far from it. I shall not bore you with too long a discussion on this issue but all you need to do is take another and deeper look around you. I am sure you'll see what I am talking about.

And as for our human moral responsibilities, the only thing we could do is what we "think" is the best and the rightest thing to do. We could punish wrong doings, we could ignore them, or we could educate the wrong doers, if there is any rationale, time, justification, budget, and all other necessary means of giving such educations. We could ignore wrong doings in our societies or we could try to cure the problems from their roots. We could be caring, sympathetic, and compassionate creatures and solve our social problems with care, empathy, kindness, and benevolence, or we could be just the opposite of these. Like everything else, whatever we do in this respect too, is what we were supposed to do. They just *happen* to have the "appearance" of freely made decisions and free behaviors. Regardless though, we will be pleased with them because it'll at least *feel* like we did a good deed because we *chose* so. But also remember, the result of doing a good deed is good, no matter how we came about doing it.

So, with all of its extreme importance, there may be no clear-cut answers to the "No-Freewill/Morality" issues. But just because those questions exist (and we can't find some all-satisfying answers for them) we should not brush the deterministic and the no-choice nature of the Universe under the carpet. It may create big enough a bump that may make somebody who is walking on that carpet, but has his eyes still in the Schroc's box, stumble and fall. And just remember:

"What Happens Is What Was Supposed to Have Happened!"

NOTES

[1] In computer and digital technologies, "bit" is the basic unit of information which takes values of either 0 or 1, and therefore, is a binary quantity (see also Chapter 6 under *4. Concentration*). In fact, the word "bit" is a portmanteau for "**b**inary" "dig**it**".

[2] The insertion of the phrase "at least informationally" is because somethings may be connected or interconnected physically as well.

NAME INDEX

Alpher, Ralph 7
Atkins, Peter 3
Becquerel, Henri 146
Berzelius, Jons Jakob 53
Bohm, David 190, 192, 194, 198
Bohr, Neils 125, 149-50, 157-8, 163, 165-6
Boltzmann, Ludwig 148
Bondi, Hermann 11
Born, Max 6, 24, 124, 151-2, 164, 169-70, 172, 176, 206-7
Bose, Satyendra Nath 27
Bruns, Heinrich 139
Carnot, Sadi 145
Compton, Arthur 153
Crick, Francis 91, 98, 105
Crum-Brown, Alexander 99
Curie, Marie 146, 165
Curie, Pierre 146
Davisson, Clinton 150

de Broglie, Louis 149, 190, 192, 194
Democritus 126
Descartes, René 127, 199
Dizikes, Peter 142, 144
Doroshkevich, Andrei 7
Einstein, Albert 26-7, 48, 125, 147-9, 165, 190
Emerson, Ralph Waldo 125
Fermi, Enrico 127
Feynman, Richard 145
Fraser, Thomas 99
Fuller, Richard Buckminster 197
Gerhardt, Charles Frédéric 100
Germer, Lester 150
Gold, Thomas 11, 82
Hawking, Stephen 11, 54, 125, 196, 198
Heisenberg, Werner 152, 157-8, 162, 165-6

Heitler, Walter   45
Herman, Robert   7
Honderich, Ted   126
Hoyle, Fred   12, 14
Hubble, Edwin   5, 11, 14
Hund, Friedrich   45
Huygens, Christiaan   146
Jordan, Pascual   152
Joule, James Prescott   145
Kajita, Takaaki   30
Kepler, Johannes   136
Khayyam, Hakim Omar   125
Kirchhoff, Gustav   147
Klechkovsky, Vsevolod   33
Laplace, Pierre-Simon   127, 135, 162
Leibniz, Gottfried   125, 137, 141
Lemaitre, Georges H.J.E.   5, 7, 11-12, 14, 173
Lennard-Jones, John   46
Leucippus   126
Lewis, Gilbert N.   163
Li, T.Y.   143
London, Fritz   45
Lorenz, Edward   139-144
Madelung, Erwin   33-5, 37
Maxwell, James Clerk   146
McDonald, Arthur B.   30
Mendeleev, Dmitri   20, 23
Michelson, Albert   146-7, 165
Miescher, Friedrich   79
Mlodinow, Leonard   196, 198
Morley, Edward   146-7, 165
Mulliken, Robert S.   18, 46
Newton, Isaac   25, 126, 136-141, 144-5, 151, 153, 162, 196
Novikov, Igor   7
Occam (or Okham), William of   1
Oscar II, King   139
Pauli, Wolfgang   31, 38, 166
Pauling, Linus   41, 45, 54, 105
Penzias, Arno   7, 14
Planck, Max   38, 147-9, 165, 172
Poincaré, Henri   139, 141-2, 144
Rutherford, Ernest   146, 149
Schrödinger, Erwin   18, 32, 38, 46, 82, 98, 150-1, 159-61, 165-6, 190, 192, 198
Seena, Abu Ali   107
Slater, John C.   46
Soddy, Frederick   146
Spinoza, Baruch   125, 167
Thomson, J.J.   146
Thomson, William (Lord Kelvin)   145-6, 165
von Mayer, Julius Robert   145
von Meyer, Julius Lothar   20
Watson, James   105, 120
Wiedemann, E.E.G.   51
Wilson, Robert   7, 14
Yorke, James   142
Young, Thomas   153

SUBJECT INDEX

Acid, deoxyribonucleic (DNA) 79-91, 93, 95-8, 102, 105-6
Acid, ribonucleic (RNA) 88-90, 92, 95, 102
Acids, amino 58, 60, 63, 91-2, 94, 98, 117
Acids, carboxylic 56
Acids, nucleic 58, 61, 79, 87-9, 102
Adenine 77-8, 80
Alphabet, atomic 76
Amines 56
Amygdala 110, 115
Anticodon 91-4
Aspirin 100
Atomic number 21, 41
Atomic orbitals 32-3, 45, 50, 169
Aufbau principle, the 30-1, 33-6
Base, nucleic 77, 79-81, 83, 87-91, 102
Bases, complementary 77, 79-81, 83, 87-91, 102
Big Bang xiii, xix, 3-7, 9-12, 48-9, 123, 164, 169, 172-4, 179-84, 186, 189, 199-201
Causality 124, 126, 183, 187
Cerebellum 111, 120
Cerebrum 109, 111
Chaos theory xx, 127, 136, 139, 141-4, 171-2, 188, 191
Chemical reactivity 29-30
Chromosome 85, 113
Codon 91, 93-4
Compatibilism 125
Copenhagen interpretation (CI) 157-61, 172, 190, 192, 194
Cosmic Background Explorer (COBE) satellite 9, 11
Cosmic Microwave Background (CMB) Radiation 7-9, 11, 49

Covalent bond(s)   29, 43-5, 53, 55, 57
Cytosine   77, 80
Dark energy   13, 16
Dark matter   13, 16
de Broglie-Bohm theory   190, 192, 194
Deoxyribonucleotide   77-8
Determinism   xiii, xiv, xx, 72, 124-34, 142, 162, 168, 171, 181, 188-90, 192-5, 200, 205
Determinism, Causal   128-31, 135, 142, 168, 181, 200
Determinism, Nomological   128
Determinism, Physical   132-3
Determinism, Soft   125
DNA   see "Acid, deoxyribonucleic"
Double helix   81, 83, 88-90
Double-Slit experiment, the   153-4, 156, 159, 164, 194
Duality, Energy-Information (EID)   xxi, 180, 182, 184, 199
Duality, wave-particle   150, 153, 156
Dynamical systems   141-2, 189
Electromagnetism   25, 28, 43, 145
Electronegativity   41-2, 54
Electropositivity   41
Elementary Particles   18, 27-8, 31

Energy Exchange Processes   184
Epigenetics   116, 122
Excited state   50-1, 163
Fatalism   130-2, 135, 181
Fermions   27-8, 31
Fragmentary model   174
"g" factor   113
Gene expression   85-6, 113, 116
Genes   xiv, 29, 84-5, 90, 95, 102, 107, 113-15, 119, 121-3, 131, 170
Gravitational lensing   26
Gravity   25-6, 28, 48, 50, 136, 145, 169, 186
Ground state   50-2, 163
Guanine   77, 80
Hemoglobin   61-3
Hippocampus   110, 120
Homo sapiens   xvii, 4, 20, 124, 187
Hydrogen bonds   57, 59, 80-1, 83, 87, 91, 174
Hydrogen-to-helium ratio   7, 9, 11
Hypothalamus   111
Incompatibilism   125
Information, threads of   179
Universal Spider Web Interconnectivity (USWI)   201, 204
Interpretation, Bohm's   190

Interpretation, Causal   190
Interpretation, Copenhagen
    157-61, 172, 190, 192, 194
Ionic bonding   41
Karma   125, 135
Lepton   30
Letters, atomic   76-7
Mass number   21
Microbiota   116-17
Molecular Orbital Theory
    (MOT)   45-6, 52
Monoamine oxidase A
    (MAOA)   114-15, 121
Mt. Wilson Observatory   5
Myoglobin   61-3
Necessitarianism   128
Neuroplastin (NPTN)   113-14, 121
Nucleosynthesis   10, 24
Nucleotide   77-82, 87-8, 90-3, 95, 121
Orbitals, atomic   18-19, 32-4, 36, 43, 45-7, 50-52, 169
Orbitals, molecular   45, 52, 57
Pauli Exclusion Principle   31
Peptide bonds   59, 197
Periodic Table, the   20-3, 35, 38, 41, 43, 65, 82, 169, 172, 184
Peripheral factors   64-6, 69
Photoelectric effect   147-8
Pilot-Wave Theory   190-1

Predeterminism   128, 130-2, 181
Psyche   109, 119
Quantitative Structure-Activity
    Relationship (QSAR)   99-101, 106
Quantum number   33
Quantum theory   4, 149, 151, 157, 161, 166, 172, 192-4, 198
Quark   28
Radiation, blackbody   147, 149
Radiation, electromagnetic   15, 16, 148, 180
Replication   102
RNA   see "Acid, Ribonucleic"
RNA, messenger   87, 90
RNA, ribosomal (rRNA)   92
RNA, transfer (tRNA)   92-4
Singularity   xix-xxi, 6, 156, 164, 173-4, 177, 179, 182-3
Small Bang   174-81, 192
Spacetime   169, 189
Spin   31-3, 44, 46
Steady State theory   11
Strong nuclear force   24-6, 28
Symmetry   7, 47-50, 54
Temperament   107-9, 112-13, 116-18, 120
Tendril   102-3, 106, 185
Thalamus   111-12
Thermonuclear reaction   179
Threshold Membrane   195-6

Thymine   77, 80, 87-8, 106
Transcription   86-90, 97-8, 102
Translation (genetic)   86, 90, 93, 98, 102
Uncertainty principle   152, 162, 166, 172
Uracil   77, 87-8
Valence Bond Theory, VBT   45-6
Valence electrons   20, 29, 41, 43, 45, 50
Walking droplet experiment   189, 191, 194
Wave function collapse   159, 190, 195
Weak nuclear force   25-6
X-rays   15, 153

Made in the USA
Monee, IL
31 May 2023

35004709R00142